GULAG

TOMASZ KIZNY

GULAG

SOLOVKI
THE WHITE SEA CANAL
THE VAIGACH EXPEDITION
THE THEATER IN THE GULAG
KOLYMA
VORKUTA
THE ROAD OF DEATH

FIREFLY BOOKS

A FIREFLY BOOK

Published by Firefly Books Ltd. 2004

Publisher Cataloging-in-Publication Data (U.S.)

Kizny, Tomasz.
    Gulag / Tomasz Kizny.
Originally published: Paris, Éditions Balland / Éditions Acropole, 2003
[496] p. : col. photos., maps ; cm.
Includes index.
Summary: A historical photographic record of the Soviet Gulag and its legacy.
ISBN 1-55297-964-4
1. Concentration camps— Russia (Federation)—History— Pictorial works. 2. Forced labor — Russia (Federation) — History— Pictorial works. 3. Prisons — Russia (Federation) — History — Pictorial works. I. Title.
365/.45/094709041 21   HV9715.15 .K59 2004

National Library of Canada Cataloguing in Publication

Kizny, Tomasz, 1958-
    Gulag : life and death inside the Societ concentration camps,
1917-1990 / Tomasz Kizny.

Translation of: Goulag
ISBN 1-55297-964-4

1. Political prisoners–Soviet Union–Pictorial works.
2. Concentration camps–Soviet Union–Pictorial works.
3. Soviet Union–Social conditions–Pictorial works.
4. Soviet Union–History–1925-1953–Pictorial works. I. Title.

DK267.K5913 2004   365'.45'09470222   C2004-902807-3

Published in the United States in 2004 by
Firefly Books (U.S.) Inc.
P.O. Box 1338, Ellicott Station
Buffalo, New York 14205

Published in Canada in 2004 by
Firefly Books Ltd.
66 Leek Crescent
Richmond Hill, Ontario L4B 1H1

Published originally under the title *Goulag*
© 2003 Editions Balland/Editions Acropole, Paris

Translated from the Polish by Antonia Lloyd-Jones.

Printed in France

The Publisher acknowledges the financial support of the Government of Canada through the Book Publishing Industry Development Program for its publishing activities.

The camp hospital. Vorkuta, 1945.

CONTENTS

ACKNOWLEDGMENTS

My project on the Gulag took seventeen years to complete, with interruptions. It began in 1986, when, in Poland, I met former inmates from the Gulag and discovered that they had kept photographs from there, and ended in 2003, when the work on this book was completed. Clearly I could not have worked on this project for so many years without the support and assistance of many people.

First of all, from the bottom of my heart, I wish to thank my parents, Anna-Maria, and my daughter Agata, who kindly put up with my continual absences and who supported me through the difficult moments.

I can't find the words to express my gratitude to Dominique Roynette. Without her stubbornness and enormous work, this book would never have appeared in this form.

I would especially like to thank Mrs. Wanda Kialka, a former inmate of the Soviet camps, for letting me use her husband Stanislaw's photographs and for her kind assistance over several years.

I wish to warmly thank Joanna Szcesna for the many hours she devoted to helping me edit texts. Also assisting me with their invaluable advice and comments were Katarzyna Madon-Mitzner, Piotr Mitzner and Anna Bikont.

Between 1986 and 1989 my project benefited from the unselfish assistance of Danuta Blahut-Bieganska, Andrzej Luc and Anna Los, friends who created Niezalezna Agencja Fotograficzna Dementi (Independent Photographic Agency Dementi) whose work was banned by Polish Communist censorship.

From 1986 to 1981, I was able to continue working on this project thanks to the kindness and financial assistance of Jerzy Giedroyc of Kultura, the Institut littéraire de Maisons-Laffitte (Literary Institute in Maisons Laffitte); Irena Lasota of the Institute for Democracy for Eastern Europe; and Andrzej Oseka of the Independent Culture Committee, Warsaw.

My two expeditions to the Road of Death in 1990 and 1991 would not have been possible without the assistance and personal participation of Alexandr Vologodsky and Erik Ivanov.

From 1992 to 1998, I worked on my project with the assistance of the Karta Center in Warsaw. I wish to thank the president of the center, Zbigniew Gluza, who included it as a research project and thus assured its financing, as well as Tomasz Gleb, a loyal friend whom I have had the pleasure to work with.

In Russia, from 1992 to 1995, I worked with Tatiana Kossinova of the Memorial Center for Scientific Information and Enlightenment in St. Petersburg, who assisted me greatly and diligently collected information, documentary photographs, and helped me contact former Gulag inmates, In addition, she organized my trips to the Solovki Islands, the White Sea Canal, and Kolyma.

In Russia, during all the years that I worked on the Gulag project, I could always count on assistance from Sergei Krivenko, Susanna Pechuro and Alexandr Gurianov of the Memorial Center for Scientific Information and Enlightenment in Moscow.

During my three trips to Vorkuta, I received a great deal of assistance from Vitaly Trochin and Evgenia Khaidorova of Vorkuta Memorial.

I wish to thank very much Yury Brodsky for allowing me to use many archival photographs from his work Solovki, *Dvadtsat' let ossobogo naznachenia (Solovki. Twenty Years of Special Purpose)*, published in Moscow in 2002 (Rossiiskaia Politicheskaia Entsyklopedia).

I would also like to thank Denis Bourgeois for all the trust that he put in me during the development of this book.

Memorial is an association born during the social democratic movement that arose in the USSR in 1988. It now consists of 86 organizations in Russia and in countries of the former Soviet Union. Its task is to discover and disseminate the historical truth about the totalitarian Soviet regime, to preserve the memory of and rehabilitate its victims, and to help former prisoners, in different ways.

Memorial also engages in various activities aimed at creating a civil society based on the rule of law in Russia. The association sets up educational programs for young people and prepares reports on human rights violations in the Russian Federation, especially in Chechnya, and in countries of the former Soviet Union.

"What I saw, no man should see or even know about.
But once he has seen it, better that he die quickly."

Varlam Shalamov, *Kolyma Tales*
Translated by John Glad

Norman Davies • British historian and writer.

GULAG, like GLASNOST or PERESTROIKA, is one of those curious terms which seem to make Russian history more colourful for foreigners. It entered general circulation via Alexander Solzhenitsyn's novel *The Gulag Archipelago*; and its origin as an acronym for the Soviet Union's "Chief Camp Administration" is quite widely known. Yet it is largely devoid of the horrific emotional charge that is carried by similar terms such as 'Nazi concentration camp' or "The Killing Fields" of Pol Pot. What is more, the names of the major sites administered by the Gulag—Solovki, Belomor, Vorkuta, Vaigach or Kolyma—mean nothing to most educated outsiders. Their ranking in the conventional catalogue of human misery in the 20th century remains peripheral. Most people would be amazed to learn that they accounted for far more human victims than Ypres, the Somme, Verdun, Auschwitz, Majdanek, Dachau and Buchenwald put together.

The reasons for this complacency are manifold. For one thing, though the Gulag functioned from the 1920s to the 1980s, the true extent and nature of this operation stayed a well-guarded secret even in Russia itself. Systematic descriptions and statistics did not begin to emerge until the Krushchev era, when the worst excesses, including the widespread use of slave labour, were abandoned. For another, a well-entrenched body of politically motivated Sovietologists had consistently denied both the scale and the murderous nature of Soviet political repressions. Most importantly perhaps, Western opinion, which has been thoroughly (and rightly) educated in the horrors of the Nazi Holocaust, is reluctant to accept and digest information about mass crimes committed by a regime which was the ally of the western powers in the war against Hitler. Indeed, a vocal segment of that opinion objects to any sort of comparisons being made between the Gulag and the Holocaust.

Of course, the Nazi KL system and the Soviet Gulag displayed important differences as well as many similarities. The former, for example, contained a number of dedicated death-camps, like Treblinka, Sobibór and Belzec where the great majority of inmates were killed on arrival. Nazi Germany also ran a chain of camps for POWs on the Eastern Front, where no provision was made for the prisoners' food, shelter or employment. The Gulag, in contrast, consisted of a far vaster network of concentration camps spread across the most northerly reaches of Europe and Asia which were officially designated as places of work. Like Auschwitz, they were often entered through a triumphal arch advocating the benefits of dedicated labor.

The standard Russian slogan *cherez trud domoi* was a forerunner and a close equivalent of the notorious German *arbeit macht frei*. Mass exterminations in the Soviet Union, which were commonplace under Stalin were generally carried out by shooting in prisons or forests and by other branches of the security services. The only so-called death-camps within the Gulag system were installations in uranium mines or nuclear power stations where unprotected workers could not expect to live for long. Work was essential to the Gulag concept. Even so, the reality was such that as often as not guests of the Great White Bear would perish, and perish in extreme distress. The harshness of the Arctic climate, the starvation levels of the diet, the length of the sentences, the punitive character of the work norms, the routine brutality and depravity of the guards, the absence of proper medical care or of adequate heating and clothing, and the lack of hope inevitably produced a devastating mortality rate. Tens of millions of the *zeks* or convicts, whether so-called politicals or criminals, were frozen, starved, worked, beaten, or dispirited to death. Some of the young, healthy and resilient ones learned to survive. But their average expectation of life did not exceed one winter. Over the decades, the Gulag presided over more human death and misery than any of its rivals.

Given the cloak of secrecy that surrounded the Gulag for so long, an extensive photographic record is not something to readily expect. But by patient research and the determined exploration of former sites, Tomasz Kizny has assembled a remarkable collection of images. He was greatly assisted both by members of the Russian Memorial Association and by survivor groups, who since the Soviet collapse are now able to function openly. The pictures range from official archival snapshots featuring both inmates and their self-important captors to scenes of colossal construction projects or of snowbound ruins, and portraits of survivors now eking out their final years in penury. Surprisingly perhaps, many survivors still live in the shadow of their former camps. With no relatives and nowhere to return to, they have been condemned indefinitely to an icy exile.

Kizny has made good use of many photographs found in Poland. Poles made up a large contingent of the Gulag's inflow in 1939-41 and again in 1944-48. They also made up one of the few categories to be allowed to leave the USSR at the end of their sentences. Some of them were sufficiently enterprising to obtain the use of a camera on release, and, exceptionally, to smuggle their photographs out with them.

It is difficult to say which pictures make the greatest impression. One might choose the panorama shots of the worksites by the White Sea Canal with the antlike figures scurrying among the gigantic seas of mud and scaffolding. One might try to look into the face and mind of Matvei Berman, head of the Gulag administration in 1932, and to imagine what he and his colleagues were thinking. Or one might want to reflect on Kizny's recent shot of a wrecked and snowbound locomotive still in place on the "Road of Death," which was supposed to link two Arctic ports 700 miles apart, and which, despite the loss of countless construction workers was never completed. Much of the work in the Gulag was not just hopeless. It was pointless.

The one picture that is missing and that, in the pre-flash era, could not be easily taken concerns a regular sight in all the camps of the Gulag. It would show huge stacks of emaciated corpses, frozen solid, piled high and wrapped in rags, awaiting the end of the Arctic night and the brief chance of the thaw and of anonymous burial.

Prisoners on their way to the camp. Karelian-Finnish Republic, 1940.

The camp at Molotov (Severodvinsk), 1946.

Jorge Semprum • former member of the resistance deported
to Buchenwald, former Spanish minister of culture,
writer, member of the Académie Goncourt

"I freely acknowledge that Soviet state policy is in the hands of an extraordinary man. Before the war, when our communist comrades would speak of the "genius of Stalin," I was inclined to smile and today I admit I was wrong. Stalin is a man of genius. What he has accomplished over the past twenty years in establishing his power, in organizing, defending and ensuring victory for his country implies exceptional talent of the kind that put a Richelieu, Cromwell, Cavour at the center stage of History. His genius is measured by magnitude, by the inner strength of efficiency and by the patient depth of his planning..."

As surprising as it may seem today, the author of this panegyric was Léon Blum. On July 21, 1945, a few weeks after returning from a deportation camp in Germany and after reassuming his leadership role in the Socialist party, Léon Blum published the lines quoted above in an article in *Le Populaire*[1] on Stalin's policy. For some time, in preparation for the 37th SFIO Congress, Léon Blum had devoted his daily column to issues concerning the unity of the worker's cause. And it was in this context that he expressed his opinion about Stalin and Soviet policy.

Blum had never shown, however, a weakness for or fascination with either communist ideas or Soviet power. At the Congress of Tours, it was Blum who opposed the Socialists adopting Lenin's draconian conditions for admission to the Third International. It was Blum's speeches— portentous if not prophetic regarding the long-term future of a party without internal democracy that had a decisive impact on the militants maintaining a substantial minority in the "Old House" of socialism. It was Blum the leader--his theoretical and practical endeavours throughout the 1920s and 1930s—who was responsible for rebuilding the SFIO and making it again the main party of the left. It was Blum, the architect of the Popular Front, who was the first head of a united leftist government (the factions were probably more thrown together than deeply united, but that's another issue!)

It was Blum whom the sinister Xavier Vallat—the future head of Jewish Affairs in the Vichy government—addressed on June 6, 1936, during the inaugural session of the Chamber of Deputies: "Your coming to power, Mr. President of the Council, unquestionably marks a historic date. For the first time, this old Gallo-Roman country will be governed by a Jew!"

[1]The French Socialist Party newspaper.

Léon Blum, then, the man who, imprisoned by Petain after the trial at Riom, wrote the essay *A l'échelle humain (For All Mankind)*, which may be considered a charter of socialism, announced on July 21, 1945, that Stalin was a man of genius who should be placed on the same level as Richelieu, Cromwell, or Cavour.

Why should we remember Blum's opinion—his error, blindness, panegyric—all difficult to understand today, especially because they came from one of the most lucid and intellectually primed political minds of the 20th century? Because Léon Blum's blindness is significant, in some ways emblematic of the attitude of the French Left, including its non-Leninist trends and currents that endured for decades.

In actual fact, we would have to wait for Khrushchev's famous secret speech to the 20th Russian Communist Party Congress, especially for Alexander Solzhenitsyn's explosive testimony several years later for the wall of silence surrounding the Gulag—or rather the Western wall of deafness—to start crumbling.

This was only the beginning, however.

Krushchev's speech was undoubtedly partial and inadequate in terms of an analysis of the whole, but overwhelmingly true; many specialists did not find it very convincing because it was not very Marxist. It was not enough to be true; it also had to follow the party line, meet the requirements of dialectical analysis, of correct thinking. As for Solzhenitsyn, he could not be trusted, could he? He was nothing but a reactionary Old Believer!

The road was long, in any case, and there were many ideological obstacles to overcome for the truth about the Soviet Union, its repressive historical essence, to finally take hold.

Be that as it may, in July 1945, when Léon Blum praised Soviet policy in general, and Stalin in particular, mass repression, which had reached its height in 1937 and then relaxed somewhat during the war effort against Nazi Germany, started anew.

To give one example, Soviet citizens incarcerated in Nazi camps were not liberated when Hitler's regime collapsed. The vast majority of survivors were sent directly to Soviet camps in the Gulag archipelago: directly from Buchenwald or Dachau to the camps of Kolyma. We can find a moving record of this atrocious fate in *Tales of Kolyma* by Varlam Shalamov, undoubtedly the greatest writer of the concentration camp experience—Nazi or Soviet—in the 20th century.

In 1945, it was the heroism of the Russian people in the war against the Nazis and the images of Stalingrad and of Soviet soldiers hoisting the red flag of victory over the ruins of the Reichstag that made it possible to maintain and spread the great lie about the shadowy realities of Stalinist society.

These heroes could not be guilty. A socialist system that had produced so many heroes could not produce executioners: that was the misleading premise. The popular prestige that the Soviet system gained throughout the world in the victory over Nazism—in which it had played a decisive role—largely explains, even if it justifies nothing, the mass obliteration of the crimes of Stalinism in the collective conscience and memory of western societies, and of French society in particular.

It also explains Léon Blum's opinion cited above and the conciliatory attitude of the Allies at the Yalta Conference, starting with Roosevelt's advisors and the American president himself.

In the 1940s, it was, then, the heroism the Russian people had displayed during the war against fascism that enabled the Soviet propaganda apparatus in all communist parties of the West to deflect public opinion or subject it to a kind of moral blackmail that increased in certain countries, Italy and France in particular, the enormous influence, the specific force, which created the intellectual terrorism, more or less widespread, of the communist parties of the post-war and cold-war era. Ten years earlier, in the 1930s, ideological mechanisms and different policies, but of a similar nature, had played the same role.

Here we must no doubt remember, even briefly and at the risk of oversimplifying, certain historical facts. It was in 1929 that stalinization of Soviet society began. After the interim of confusion and factionalism that had followed Lenin's death, Stalin, having deployed with brutal skill his "inner strength of efficiency" and "patient depth of planning," to quote Blum's extraordinary euphemism, politically removed his main opponents from the Russian Politburo. A few years later, his absolute power definitively established, he would eliminate them physically.

Economically, socially and politically, by bringing into line or forcibly disbanding soviets or trade unions, banning factions in the party, the pre-Stalinist work had been undertaken by Lenin himself—Stalin's new project was characterized by two concurrent actions filled with dire consequences.

On the one hand, Stalin eliminated NEP, the New Economic Policy Lenin had launched to re-activate, in the unbridled collectivism of the civil war era, the essential mechanisms of a market economy. These were certainly limited under state control of foreign trade, but they had an immediate positive impact on the country's economy, which suddenly revived, revitalized, and regaining a cycle of expansion.

Stalinism is therefore unthinkable without the elimination of an economy. It would be worthwhile to remind those who today claim to have devised an anti-globalization strategy against the *tyranny of the market*; to remind them that the Bolshevik's destruction of the market economy—no one anywhere would ever rival the consistency, determination, and extremism of their strategy—led to the greatest economic, social, and human catastrophe of the 20th century. Thus, in 1929, Stalin abolished NEP and launched collectivization in the rural areas, which culminated in the annihilation of the Russian peasant class through planned famines and mass deportations. At the same time, through the five-year plans, Stalin organized the forced and fanatical industrialization of Old Russia.

This inhuman undertaking, whose mortifying truth would be revealed only much later, in the international consensus—both military and civilian—of cold war and peaceful co-existence, was first perceived throughout the world as a kind of epic.

We have only to reread the poetry written at the time—in French by Louis Aragon, in Spanish by Rafael Albert, in German by Bertold Brecht, and in Russian by Vladimir Maiakovsky— to appreciate the extent and the excess of the situation.

But it was not just the poets.

Even distinguished sociologists, political scientists and economists from all countries and ideological persuasions were struck dumb, sometimes with admiration, sometimes with doubt, but they were always filled with curiosity about the enormous accomplishments, at least on a quantitative scale, of the successive five-year plans.

This can be easily explained. In 1929, when, under Stalin's instigation and at a human and social cost whose negative consequences would become obvious only much later, the USSR took the first steps towards a modern industrial society, the capitalist world was shaken by the general and prolonged crisis that followed the catastrophe of Wall Street's Black Thursday.

Under these circumstances, what vision of the world could not only the people and political militants have, but also the intellectuals and democratic circles of power? On the one hand, we have a growing USSR—the elimination of unemployment, significant rates of annual growth, real transformation, although slow and unequal, of an often archaic Russian rural society, the massive spread of secondary and university education—a genuine cultural revolution.

On the other, we find the capitalist world: rising unemployment that significantly destroyed or weakened the social fabric; the accelerated impoverishment of workers and the lower strata of the middle classes; the subsequent radicalization of all of these levels of society, which turned away from a parliamentary democracy incapable of opposing the crisis and its ensuing corruption and paved the way for fascism under various guises. On the one hand, Soviet society living by a slogan whose truth was nothing but propaganda. "Today is better than yesterday and not quite as good as tomorrow"—whose optimistic tone was reflected in film, in Eisenstein's *The General Line*, for example. On the other, the confusion and anguish of tomorrow: the existential darkness reflected in Fritz Lang's M and John Ford's *The Grapes of Wrath*.

But the progress of the Soviet Union, real to be sure, remained fragile, superficial. At heart, the country still remained a prisoner of constraints, of the impotence of backwardness. By the mid-1930s, after the superhuman efforts of the first five-year plan, the country needed to pause for breath. A growing number of industrial and party cadres had rallied around Kirov, more or less openly advocating a period of respite, a new kind of NEP that would make it possible to consolidate the gains of the first period, while relaxing the ideological and police stranglehold over society.

But Stalin, aware of the danger this would pose to his absolute power—because it would objectively involve a certain *democratization* of political life—went on the offensive. In his usual brutal manner he had the secret police undertake the assignation of Kirov, attributing the crime to the Trotskyite leftist opposition, which allowed him to organize a massive purge.

It was clearly at this point that Stalin's policy became almost irrational, losing all touch with social and historical reality and apparently dominated by a perpetual and tragic leap into the future by a pathological obsession with conspiracies, hidden enemies and the imagined treachery of his closest colleagues.

From 1935 to 1939—including the most tragic of all years, 1937, which saw the disappearance of millions of citizens into the Gulag—Stalin's secret police decapitated the Red Army, the country's scientific and intellectual institutions, industrial and technological sectors, and civilian society as a whole.

In 1937, the year the wave of mass terror was unleashed on Soviet society, the Nazi authorities opened the camp at Buchenwald outside of Weimar, on Goethe's hill of Ettersburg. Eight years later, in 1945, after being liberated by General Patton's Third Army, the camp released the members of the European anti-fascist resistance from among its inmates. The last to be repatriated were the Yugoslavs in June 1945. But the camp at Buchenwald did not cease to exist. Three months later, in the fall, it was put back into service by the political police of the Soviet occupation zone in Germany. It became Speziallager No. 2, which would close only in 1950, after the creation of the German Democratic Republic.

It is therefore entirely logical that, after the democratic reunification of Germany, we now find, in the former camp at Buchenwald, two museums within the walls of the place of memory: one commemorating the Nazi camp, the other, the Stalinist camp. It is also entirely logical that a foundation, Stiftung Ettersberg, has undertaken a comparative study of the two totalitarian states that ravaged Europe in the last century.

Because one must compare, to establish historically and irrefutably, both the similarities and the differences between the two totalitarian systems, Nazism and Communism. The archipelago of the Nazi camps and the Stalin Gulag represent in effect both identical and alternate experiences. The photographs in this book make it possible to appreciate them.

It seems to me that an objective comparison of the two totalitarian systems, based on documented evidence, is the final step that must be taken to definitively end the Western blindness to the Soviet Gulag.

The camp hospital. Vorkuta, 1945.

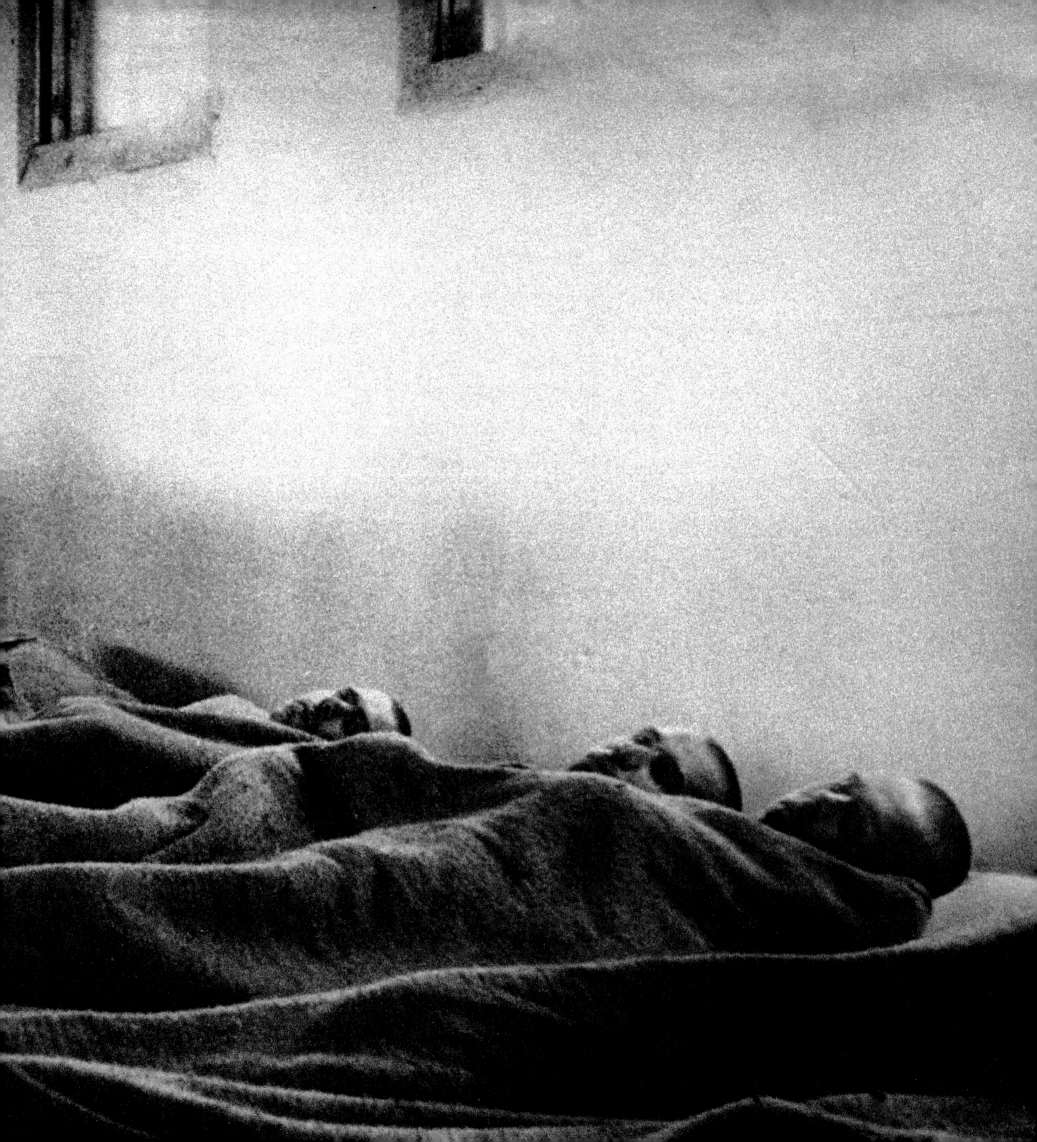

Sergeï Kovalev •former prisoner of Kolyma, Human Rights
activist in Russia •currently a deputy of the Duma

SERGEÏ KOVALEV

THE LONG SHADOW OF THE GULAG

Mass repression took a much heavier toll on human life in the USSR than the wars the country fought during the 80 years of its existence. The system that did this relied upon hatred, violence and terror affecting the whole of society, including the system's own officials, who could at any moment themselves become its victims. In Soviet Russia a dangerous combination of a slave mentality with a revolutionary one had set in. The slave-like attitude was the source of an ancient, deep-rooted sense of fear and meek compliance towards those in power, and also the popular conviction that violence is a natural prerequisite for ruling the country. By contrast, the revolutionary mind-set introduced the principle of making a ruthless effort to achieve one's goals, with no regard whatsoever for the life of the individual. It was upon these foundations that a state arose which imprisoned and murdered huge numbers of its own citizens in the name of an ideology.

The Bolsheviks created the system of prison camps and penal colonies after coming to power in 1917. First to be locked up in them were their political opponents: members of other parties and Tsarist officers. Next were simply any citizens who did not support the regime: entrepreneurs, officials, intelligentsia, the richer peasants, and priests. Finally the terror encompassed all levels of society, and communists and Cheka men (the political police) began to pour into the Gulag too. Anyone could end up "behind the wire." Because of an informer, a confession forced under torture, or simply "for nothing," anyone could be arrested as part of the NKVD's latest operation. This was decreed by the Politburo, which identified social or national groups to be "purged" and determined how many were to be arrested. From the outbreak of the Second World War citizens of countries occupied by the USSR also ended up in the Gulag camps: Lithuanians, Latvians, Estonians and Poles. After the death of Stalin, in the mid-1950s most of the foreigners and political prisoners were released from the camps. Soon, however, imprisonment of anyone "disloyal" began again: dissidents, writers, member of religious or national movements, such as Ukrainians, Tatars, or Armenians... The repression went on until the mid-1980s, when Mikhail Gorbachov initiated *perestroika*.

The Gulag is not a closed chapter in history, above all because to this day we do not know the whole truth about it. Moreover, the Gulag still exists in the Russian mentality, in its slavish manner, in its willingness to accept propaganda and lies, and in its indifference to the fate of its fellow citizens or to crimes and transgressions including those committed by the state.

In the camp we used to refer to the prisoners who kept to themselves as being "all alone on an ice floe." In social life, just as in the camp, it is important to overcome indifference and isolation. Today they take your neighbor to solitary confinement, tomorrow they'll take the other one, and next day they'll take you. You can't give the authorities licence for lawlessness — you have to protest. It might seem ineffective on the surface, but this approach does eventually put a stop to terror and abuse of power. And most importantly, it protects the individual from coercion.

The slave mentality still persists in Russia because the Soviet system was never brought to trial. There was no equivalent of the Nuremberg Trials in our country. After all, who would have had to initiate the process and carry it out? Amazingly, President Boris Yeltsin did make a faint-hearted attempt at it in 1992. The Constitutional Court was supposed to investigate whether the decision to dissolve the Soviet Communist Party, which the President had taken a year earlier, had been justified. This was when an experts' report was produced by the Memorial Society, from which it appeared that the Communist Party was a criminal organization in the USSR. And that was all. The Court did not issue an unequivocal verdict. Why not? Imagine if the denazification of Germany had been conducted by officials from the Nazi regime. What sort of result would that have produced? Nowadays all the top posts in our country are held by people from the old system, former party activists and security *apparat* employees. No one is eager to uncover the truth, and legal proceedings are quite out of the question.

On the anniversary of Stalin's death Russia's President, Vladimir Putin, reinstated the Stalinist national anthem and raised a toast. "Maybe I'm making a mistake," he said, "but I'm making the same mistake as the entire nation." And gradually, systematically, with the help of suitable legislation and pressures, the nation is being deprived of its liberty. The journalists already know what they aren't allowed to say, and the judges know the extent of their independence. These are the results of a Soviet upbringing, the long shadow of the Gulag.

I am a decided opponent of "political lustration" laws. Yet I do think that those guilty of crimes committed in the past should face prosecution, not on the basis of new penal codes, as was the case at Nuremberg, but in accordance with the law that was binding in the USSR at the time when the crimes were committed. For instance, the verdicts that caused hundreds of thousands of people to be unlawfully condemned; the judges are implicated in this. And what about the crimes perpetrated by the investigators who tortured people under arrest and brought false charges against them? They should also be brought to trial — not in order to punish or imprison them, but they should be given sentences in accordance with the supreme authority of the law, for the sake of settling the scores fairly, and to identify evil for what it is. The guilty parties could later be reprieved, or given symbolic sentences.

However, we can't count on that happening. Not just for political reasons, but also because of our mentality: we don't want to feel that we're guilty. Throughout our bloody, cruel, shameful history, it was always someone else who was guilty, whatever the crime; it was always "them" — the Jews, the Georgians, the Chechens, who did it but never us.

We didn't want to know about the Gulag, we didn't want to see it; we believed the propaganda that anyone who was arrested was an "enemy of the people." We hated them. We went out onto the streets with placards reading: "Death to the Trotskyite dogs!" We shouted out at rallies and demanded their death — huge crowds of us.

If, by some miracle, we ever finally get over that Soviet mentality, we should summon up the strength to say two little words: forgive us. Just like the Germans. Meanwhile, we're still on the lookout for someone to blame.

Of course, top responsibility for the Gulag belongs to the Communist Party, the security *apparat* and the system. Only we created that system, we, the citizens of this country.

U   S

Moscow

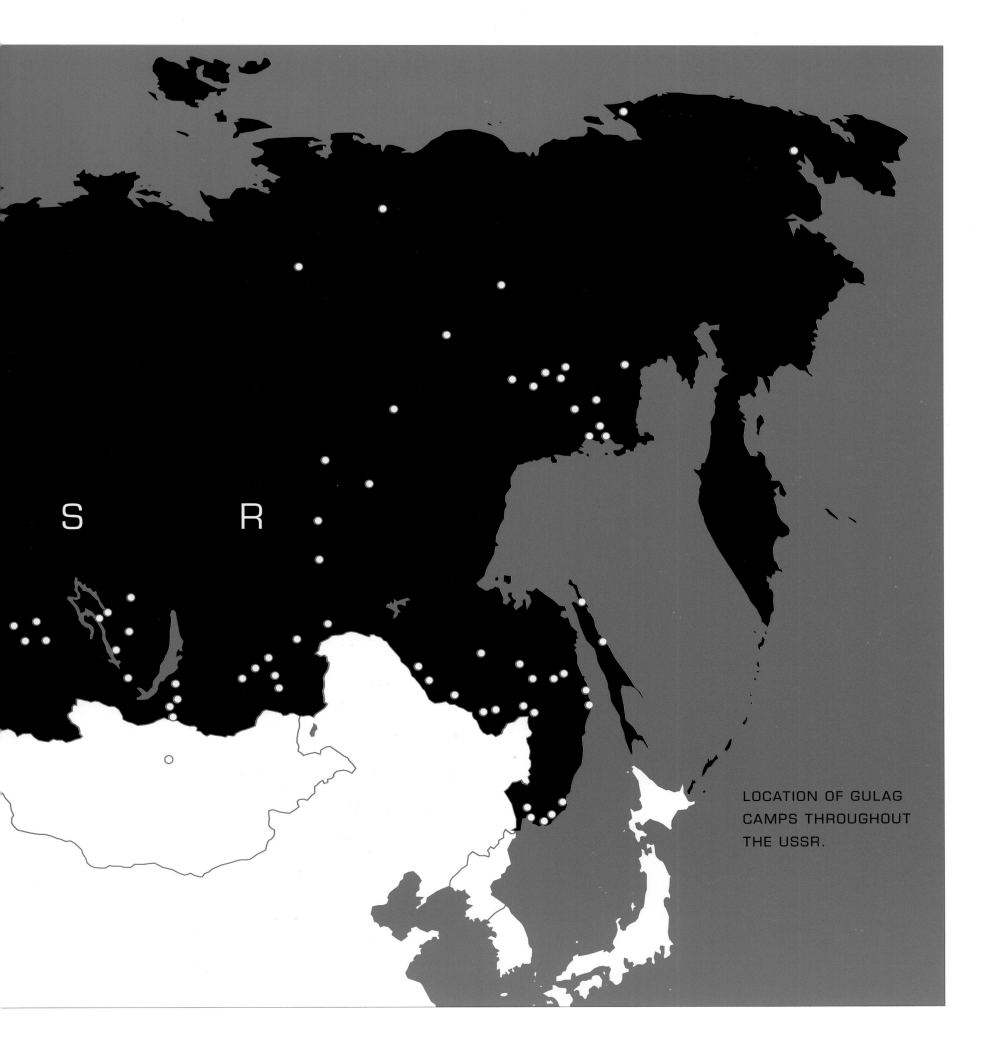

S   R

LOCATION OF GULAG
CAMPS THROUGHOUT
THE USSR.

LIST OF USSR CAMP ADMINISTRATIONS, 1923-1960

Each camp oversaw its own network of prison camps, including camps and sub-camps. These varied in number from under ten to several hundred and over the course of their existence embraced over 30,000 camp units.

The closing date of 1960 indicates that the camps still existed in that year, and probably in the next few years as well, but data about the camps, following the Gulag's dissolution on January 25, 1960, has not yet been made public.

Chief camp administrations

OGPU-NKVD-MVD Chief Administration of Camps – GULAG 25 April 1930 – 25 January 1960

Chief Administration for the Mica Industry 1950-53
Chief Camp Administration for Industrial Construction 1941-53
Chief Camp Administration for Mining and Metallurgical Enterprises 1941-53
Chief Camp Administration for Refinery and Synthetic Liquid Fuel Works Construction 1951-53
Chief Camp Administration for the Asbestos Industry 1950-53
Chief Camp Administration for the Timber Industry 1941-58
Far North Construction Administration – Dalstroi 1931-53
NKVD Camp Administration for Ironworks 1941
NKVD Fuel Industry Administration 1941
NKVD Special Construction Administration 1940-45
Special Chief Administration 1946-53
USSR MVD Chief Camp Administration for Hydroengineering Construction 1947-49
USSR MVD Chief Camp Administration for Volga-Baltic Waterway Construction 1952-53
USSR MVD Chief Camp Administration for Volga-Don Watershed Canal Construction 1949-52
USSR MVD Kuibyshevgidrostroi 1951-53
USSR MVD Sheksnagidrostroi 1951- 52
USSR MVD Special Construction Administration 1954-55
USSR MVD Sredazgidrostroi 1950-53
USSR MVD Stalingradgidrostroi 1950-53
USSR MVD Vytegorgidrostroi 1951-52
USSR NKVD Chief Administration for Airport Construction 1941-46
USSR NKVD Chief Camp Administration for Hydroengineering Construction 1940-41
USSR NKVD-MVD Chief Administration for Highways 1936-53
USSR NKVD-MVD Chief Camp Administration for Railway Construction 1940-53

Regional camp administrations

Afinatsiya Factory ITL, Krasnoiarsk 1941-51
Airport Construction Site, Moscow province 1936
Akhtubinsk ITL, Stalingrad 1950-53
Akhunlag, Krasnodar Krai 1934-35
Aktiubinlag, Kazak Republic 1940-46
Aldanlag, Yakutia Republic 1947-54
Aldan ITL within Dalstroi, Yakutia Republic 1941-43
Aldan
ITAtNo. 11, Yakutia Republic 1948-51
Alluvaistroy, Kirov province 1941
Altailag, Altai Krai 1943-45
Amgunsky ITL, Khabarovsk Krai 1946-47
Amurlag, Khabarovsk Krai 1947-53
Amur Railroad ITL, Khabarovsk Krai 1938-41
Angarlag, Bratsk, Irkutsk province 1947-60____
O
Angrenlag, Tashkent, Uzbek Republic 1945-46
Apatite Combine ITL, Murmansk province 1950-53
Aralichevlag, Kemerovo province 1951-53
Arkhbumlag, Arkhangelsk 1938-40
Arkhbumstroy, Arkhangelsk province 1940-44
Arkhperpunkt, Arkhangelsk 1931-33
Ash ITL, Moscow province 1951-53
Astrakhanlag, Astrakhan 1940-50
Atbasarsky ITL, ? 1955-56
Azovlag, Ukrainian Republic 1953
Azov ITL, Krivoy Rog, ?
Azov LOs, Republic of the Ukraine 1954-55

Bakallag, Cheliabinsk 1941-42
Bakovlag, Moscow province 1953-56
Balaganskie LOs, Irkutsk province 1949-53
Balakhlag, Nizhninovgorod Krai 1932-34
Baleylag, Chyty province 1947-53
Bamlag, Amur province 1932-38
Barashevlag, Mordvin Republic 1953-54
Bashspetsneftestroy Construction Site, Bashkirian Republic 1952-53
Baydarlag, New Port, Tiumen province 1948
Bazhenovlag, Sverdlovsk province 1950-53
Belbaltlag, Karelian-Finnish Republic 1944-45
Belogorlag, Mordovian Republic 1953-58
Belokorovitsky Prison Camp, Ukrainian Republic 1941
Belomor [White Sea]-Baltic ITL, Karelian-Finnish Republic 1931-41
Belozherskie LOs, Kuybyshev province 1951-53
Belrechlag, Murmansk province 1951-53
Berelosky GRU LO, Magadan province 1951-53
Berezlag, Arkhangelsk province 1942
Beriozovlag, Tyumen province 1948
Beriozovsky ITL, Murmansk

province 1954-56
Beriozovzoloto, Sverdlovsk province 1947-48
Berlag, Magadan, Khabarovsk Krai 1948-54
Beskudnikovskie LOs, Moscow province 1952-53
Bezymianlag, Kuybyshev province 1940-46
Birlag, Jewish Autonomous District 1939-40
Bobrovlag, Sverdlovsk 1953
Bodaibinlag, Irkutsk province 1947-54
Bogoslovlag, Sverdlovsk province 1940-53
Borlag, Chyty province 1949-51
Bratsk ITL, Irkutsk province 1946-47
Bukachachlag, Chyty province 1938-42
Burlag, Jewish Autonomous District 1938-42
Burepolomlag, Gorky province 1946-53
Buysky GES Construction Site, Yaroslavl province? 1941
BZ ITL, Moscow province 1952-53

Central Hospital LO within Dalstroi, Magadan province 1951-53
Chapayev ITL, Kuybyshev province 1944
Chaunlag within Dalstroi, Chukhotka 1951-53
Chaunchukotlag within Dalstroi, Chukhotka 1949-57
Cheboksarlag, Chuvash Republic, 1941-42
Cheliablag, Cheliabinsk 1947-51
Cheliabinsk ITL, Cheliabinsk 1943-47
Cherdaklag, Ulyanovsk province 1946-53
Cherepovetslag, Vologda province 1940-41
Chernogorlag, Krasnoiarsk Krai 1950-53
Chernogorsk Special ITL, Krasnoyarsk Krai 1944-45
Chernoistochlag, Sverdlovsk province 1942-43
Chukhotstroilag, Evgekinot, Chukhotka 1949-56
Chystiunlag, Altai Krai 1946-51
Combine No. 6 ITL, Tajik Republic 1945-46
Combine No. 7 Construction Site, Estonian Republic 1946-47
Combine No. 9 ITL, Kaliningrad province 1947-53
Construction Site 4, Karaganda, Kazak Republic 1943-44
Construction Site 6, Khabarovsk Krai 1952-53
Construction Site 16, Irkutsk 1948-53
Construction Site 18, Bashkirian Republic 1949-53
Construction Site 90, Moscow 1947-49
Construction Site 105, Murmansk province 1940-41
Construction Site 106, Murmansk province 1941
Construction Site 108, Azerbaijani Republic 1944-50
Construction Site 159, Georgian Republic 1949-50
Construction Site 210, Ukrainian Republic 1938-39
Construction Site 211, Ukrainian Republic 1938-40
Construction Site 213, Nakhodka Bay, Nadmorsky Krai 1939-41
Construction Site 247, Cheliabinsk 1949-53
Construction Site 258, Leningrad

1949-53
Construction Site 304, Cheliabinsk province 1952-53
Construction Site 313, Sverdlovsk 1949
Construction Site 442, Kaluga province 1951-53
Construction Site 447, Estonian Republic 1949-50
Construction Site 462, Dnipropetrovsk province 1951-53
Construction Site 496, Leningrad 1946-49
Construction Site 505, Mordvin Republic 1949
Construction Site 505 GULZDS, Buriat-Mongolian Republic 1947-53
Construction Site 506, Sakhalin province 1950-53
Construction Site 507, Khabarovsk Krai 1950-53
Construction Site 508, Khabarovsk Krai 1950-53
Construction Site 509, Murmansk province 1951-53
Construction Site 510, Arkhangelsk 1951-53
Construction Site 511, Murmansk 1951-53
Construction Site 513, Nadmorsky Krai 1952-53
Construction Site 514, Sverdlovsk 1953
Construction Site 514 GULZDS, Nadmorsky Krai 1952-53
Construction Site 560, Moscow 1949
Construction Site 565, Moscow 1951-53
Construction Site 585, Mordvin Republic 1949-53
Construction Site 600, Novossibirsk 1949-53
Construction Site 601, Tomsk 1949-53
Construction Site 612, Kyrgyz Republic 1951-53
Construction Site 620, Kalinin province 1949-53
Construction Site 621, Stavropol Krai 1951-53
Construction Site 665, Tajik Republic 1949-53
Construction Site 713, Moscow province 1946-49
Construction Site 770, ? 1951-52
Construction Site 791, Sukhumi 1946-49
Construction Site 833, Kalinin province 1946-49
Construction Site 859, Cheliabinsk 1946-49
Construction Site 865, Sverdlovsk province 1946-49
Construction Site 881, Perm province1946-49
Construction Site 882, Ukrainian Republic 1947-49
Construction Site 883, Uzbek Republic 1946-48
Construction Site 885, Kirov 1945-48
Construction Site 896, Tajik Republic 1947-49
Construction Site 907, Estonian Republic 1947-49
Construction Site 915, Perm province 1949-50
Construction Site 940, Ukrainian Republic 1949-53
Construction Site 994, Krasnoiarsk Krai 1950
Construction Site 1001, Kuybyshev province 1941-43
Construction Site 1418, Sverdlovsk province 1947-49
Construction Site and Tsimlan Hydrotechnical ITL

Dallag, Kazak Republic1952-54
Darasunskie LOs, village of Darasun? 1948-53
Dmitlag, Moscow province 1932-38
Dmitrov Machinery Plant ITL, Moscow province 1938-40
Dmitrov Region GULAG Construction Site, ? 1938
Donlag, ? 1946-47
DS Yeniseystroy ITL, Krasnoyarsk 1951-52
DT ITL, Moscow province 1952-53
Dubogorlag, Dvorets station on the Kalinin railroad, 1953-57
Dubravlag, Mordvin Republic 1948-60
DYu ITL, Moscow province 1952-53
Dzhezkazganlag, Kazak Republic 1940-43
Dzhugdzhurlag, Yakutsk 1947-53
Dzhydynlag, Buriat-Mongolian Republic 1941-49

Eastern ITL, Nadmorsky Krai 1943-47
Eastern Lead Mines Administration, Krasnoiarsk Krai? 1950-52
Elgen LO within Dalstroi, Magadan province 1951-53

Far-eastern ITL, Khabarovsk 1929-39

Gagarlag, Crimea province 1953-55
GA ITL, Moscow province 1952-53
GB ITL, Moscow province 1952-53
Gdovlag, Slantsy station on the Leningrad railroad 1940-41
Glazovlag, Udmurt Republic 1954-55
Gorlag, Norilsk 1948-54
Gornoshorlag, Akhpun station on the Tomsk railroad 1938-41
Granitovy ITL, Krasnoiarsk Krai 1950
Gurlag, Kazak Republic 1943
Gusinoozerlag, Buriat-Mongolian Republic 194-42

Highway ITL within Dalstroi, Magadan province 1951-54

Ilimsky Special ITL, Irkutsk province 1955-56
IN ITL, Moscow province 1952-53
Indygirka ITL within Dalstroi, Yakutia Republic 1949-58
Intlag, Komi Republic 1941-48
ITL attached to Oboronstroi, Karelian-Finnish Republic 1941
ITL No. 4 GUSZOSDOR, Yaroslavl province 1944-45
ITL PO Box 4, Krasnoiarsk 1951
Ivdellag, Sverdlovsk province 1937-60

Kachov ITL, Stalingrad province 1949-53
KA ITL, Moscow 1952-53
Kaluga ITL, Kaluga 1936-38
Kamienlag, Novossibirsk 1953-55
Kamiensk ITL, Saratov province 1942-44
Kamyshlag, Kemerovo province 1951-54
Kandalaksha ITL, Murmansk province 1940-41
Karagandaugol, Kazak Republic 1943-44
Karagandinstroi, Kazak Republic 1946-48
Karakumlag, Karakalpak Republic

1950-53
Karlag, Kazak Republic 1931-59
Kazan Crude Oil Refinery Construction Site, Tatar Republic 1952-53
Khabarlag, Khabarovsk, 1939-43
Khakaskie LOs, Krasnoiarsk Krai, 1947-53
Khakasslag, Bashkirian Republic 1953-55
Khimkovsk Camp Section, Moscow 1942-44
Khimlag, Moscow, 1939-41
Krasnoiarsk Construction Site, Krasnoiarsk 1949-51
Krasnoiarsk-Yeniseysk Railroad Line Construction Site, Krasnoiarsk 1952-53
Kargopollag, Arkhangelsk province 1937-60
Kaspilag, Astrakhan, Baku 1943-46
Kazlag, Alma-Ata, Kazak Republic 1930-31
Keksholmlag, Leningrad province 1940-41
Kemerovozhilstroi, Kemerovo province 1946-48
Kimpersaylag, Kazak Republic 1941-42
Kitoylag, Irkutsk province 1947-48 and 1953-60
Kizellag, Perm province 1947-60
Kluchevlag, Chyty province 1947-48 and 1950-53
Kochkarlag, Cheliabinsk province 1947-52
Kokshynsky ITL, Altai Krai 1947
Kolag, Murmansk 1939-41
Koslanlag, Komi Republic 1954-60
Kosvinlag, Perm province 1949-50
Kotlas Agricultural LO, Arkhangelsk province 1949-56
Kotlas Despatch and Loading Point, Arkhangelsk province 1938-40
Kotlas GULZDS Department, Arkhangelsk province 1940-43
Kotlaslag, Arkhangelsk province 1943 1945
Kovrov ITL, Vladimir province 1940-41
Kraslag, Krasnoiarsk Krai 1938-60
Krasnogorlag, Sverdlovsk 1953-60
Kuloilag, Arkhangelsk 1937-42
Kunevevsky ITL, Stavropol, Kuybyshev province 1949-58
Kungur ITL, Perm province 1931
Kurianovstroi, Moscow province 1948-53
Kusyinlag, Perm province 1946-53
Kuzbaslag, Stalinsk [Novokuznetsk] 1946-48
Kuznetslag, Cheliabinsk 1953-60

Likovlag, Moscow province 1938-41
Lobvinlag, Sverdlovsk province 1943-45
Lokchimlag, Komi Republic 1937-40
Lower Amur ITL, Khabarovsk Krai 1947-55
Lower Don ITL, Rostov province, 1952-53
Lower Volga ITL, Stalingrad province 1942
Luglag, Kazak Republic 1949-51
Luzhlag, Leningrad 1937-41
Lysogorlag, Stavropol Krai 1954-55

Maglag within Dalstroi, Magadan 1951-56

"The Prison Camps. An Encyclopedic Guide", issued by the Memorial Center for Research, Information and Dissemination (NIPC) in Moscow, jointly edited by Nikita Okhotin and Arseny Roginsky.

ITL = Corrective Labor Camp
LO = Prison Camp

Solvetsky Islands

Solvetsky
Monastery

WHITE
SEA

5 km

SOLOVKI

SOLOVKI
1923 - 1939

More than any other place, the monastery on the Solovetsky Islands in the White Sea symbolizes the tragedy inflicted on Russia by the Bolshevik Revolution of 1917. In the 1920s this magnificent sanctuary of the Russian Orthodox faith was transformed into a concentration camp that launched the entire Gulag system. Solovki, as it is popularly known in Russian, witnessed the suffering of thousands of innocent people as well as the near destruction of an entire religion and many centuries of tradition. It epitomizes the ruination of Russia's spiritual and material culture in the name of communist ideology.

In October 1990, shortly after the first democratic elections in the history of the Soviet Union, a monument was erected in Moscow to the victims of Soviet totalitarianism and genocide. A huge, rough boulder was brought from the Solovetsky Islands, and placed in Lubianka Square, the site that for seven decades had inspired terror in the citizens of the Soviet Union. The stone was laid opposite the prison and the central headquarters of Soviet repression. At the time, the statue of Feliks Dzerzhinsky still stood in the square. He was the founder of the Cheka, the political police, which, later was renamed the OGPU and then the NKVD. It committed some of the greatest crimes in the history of mankind. For several months, until Dzerzhinsky's statue was removed, the two monuments stood next to each other, marking the end of an era that began with the October Revolution.

The history of Solovetsky Monastery goes back to the 15th century, when Orthodox anchorite monks chose as a place of seclusion these uninhabited islands in the White Sea, located on the northern borders of Russia. The isolation and the harsh, but also unusually beautiful, natural surroundings were conducive to contemplation and prayer. Over the following centuries a large monastery complex developed on the Solovetsky Islands. It became a masterpiece of sacred architecture and an important cultural center in Russia. The monastery developed into one of the holy places of Orthodoxy, to which thousands of believers made pilgrimages. Icons painted in the monastery's workshops adorned the churches of northern Russia, and hand-written volumes contributed to the rich Solovetsky library.

The monastery was also a major economic center. Despite the severe climate, the monks successfully bred livestock, cultivated the land, grew flowers in its hothouses and various local plants in its botanical garden. Salt was extracted from seawater, and a fleet of sailing boats that belonged to the order traded along the White Sea basin, fished, and hunted seals. Sealskins were treated at the local tannery. The monastery had its own mills, sawmills, ironworks, smithy, brickyards and pottery. The monks built a dry dock for ship repairs, a network of canals linking the lakes on the Great Solovetsky Island, and a system to supply water to the monastery. At the start of the 20th century the monastery had a hydropower plant and a radio station, and was even considering buying an airplane.

Catastrophe first struck in May 1918 when a Red Army division arrived at the monastery gates. The soldiers requisitioned the grain stock. Soon after, the Soviet authorities took over the entire monastery and established a *sovkhoz*, or state farm, on the islands. The monastery's valuables and liturgical vessels were looted, the bells were cast down, the crosses cut in two, and a red star was fixed to the top of the bell tower. In only three years under the illiterate revolutionary commissars, the monastery's economy, built up over five centuries, lay in ruins. To wipe out the evidence of their mismanagement, one of the perpetrators set a fire to the monastery that consumed part of the buildings and the church's wooden cupolas.

In 1923 the Solovetsky Special Purpose Camp was established on the islands. The churches, hermitages and monastery buildings were converted into prisoners barracks and camp administrative offices. The interiors of the churches, the iconostases, or icon screens bearing the works of mediaeval masters, and the monastery library were ransacked and later destroyed. The relics of the monastery's founders, the hermits Savvaty, Zosima and Herman, were removed from their tombs and sent to the Museum of Atheism in Leningrad. The Solovetsky monks were driven out or arrested.

Crammed into bare wooden bunks set up in the churches, the prisoners were held in appalling conditions – hungry, louse-infested and frozen. The militant atheists among the camp supervisors deliberately placed the toilets on the site of the ruined altars. The Church of the Ascension on Sekirnaia Mountain was changed into a solitary confinement block and execution site. A place once reserved for hymns and prayers was now filled with the brutality of the camp guards. Prisoners were beaten unconscious with wooden clubs, doused in water in the freezing cold and made to stand "on the stump," stripped naked and exposed to the bites of thousands of mosquitoes. The guards tortured them with senseless orders such as carrying water from one hole in the ice to another, or "counting the seagulls," which required a prisoner to shout at the top of his voice, "Seagull one, seagull two, seagull three..." and so on, until he was totally exhausted. Female prisoners were raped routinely and forced into sexual cohabitation by the camp administrators and guards.

The flower of Russian society was deported to Solovki: intellectuals, philosophers, writers, artists, scientists, political and social workers, aristocrats, Czarist officers, entrepreneurs and clergymen. This marked the second stage of a process begun with the revolution and the civil war – the systematic extermination of the Russian intelligentsia as a class enemy of the "dictatorship of the proletariat." Also arrested were peasants, craftsmen and workers, as well as common criminals and prostitutes, as part of a campaign to clean up Soviet Russia. Inmates at the Solovetsky camp died of hunger and exhaustion caused by unendurable workloads in the harsh northern climate. Over the course of the 16 years of its operation, the camp held at least 840,000 prisoners. The total number of victims has not yet been established, but certainly approaches 15,000.

At Solovki, criminal camp practices were at first hidden behind a façade of propaganda about the re-education of prisoners through labor in the name of socialism; this later became the norm throughout the Gulag. Alongside the degradation, lethal drudgery and massive death tolls, the camp created its own reality: a theater for performers, its own newspaper *Novye Solovki*, and a brass band. Portraits of Lenin and slogans reading "Labor strengthens body and soul" or "Long live free and joyful labor" were hung in the ruined churches. A film crew came from Moscow to make a rose-tinted film about life in the camp. By invitation of the authorities, the writer Maxim Gorky visited the Islands and wrote in defence of the camp an article entitled "Solovki," which was published in the Soviet and foreign press; there he not only claimed that the inmates were in good health but also praised the "educational efforts" of the OGPU.

The Solovetsky camp was a sort of laboratory for methods that would be applied for years to come throughout the Gulag system. The main focus was on finding ways to raise productivity levels among the slave laborers. These ranged from promises of early release, threatened reductions in food rations for failure to meet quotas, to incarceration in the isolation cells, and summary execution for refusal to work. It was in this context that Naftaly Frenkel, head of the agricultural department at the Solovetsky camp and later for many years a senior Gulag administrator, was to utter his famous maxim, "We must squeeze everything out of the prisoner in the first three months—after that we have no more use for him."

At first the Solovki prisoners worked only on the islands, but soon, like cancer cells, as Alexander Solzhenitsyn put it in *The Gulag Archipelago*, the labor camp system began to spread onto the mainland. New branches were opened on the White Sea coast, in Karelia, in the Urals and on the Kola Peninsula.

Established in 1930, the Chief Camp Administration, or GULAG, put all places of imprisonment under centralized management of the OGPU and initiated a huge expansion of the prison camp system throughout the Soviet Union. The number of inmates also rose dramatically. If in the 1920s forced labor was primarily intended to cover the costs of maintaining the camps, by the next decade the prisoners had began to be treated as a strategic workforce. The Gulag, run by the OGPU and later the NKVD, became an important sector in the state economy, charged with implementing many of the USSR's major industrial projects.

In 1933, after 10 years of operation, the Solovetsky camp declined in importance and was absorbed into the White Sea-Baltic camp, a larger structure within the ever expanding Gulag. It was later renamed the Solovetsky Special Purpose Prison, and finally closed down in 1939. By the time the last prisoners were removed from the ruined Solovetsky Monastery, the network of Gulag camps covered the entire territory of the Soviet Union, and the number of prisoners had reached two million.

After the closure of the camp, a naval unit was stationed on the Solovetsky Islands. The Soviet authorities took no interest in the site as a cultural monument until 1974, when the Solovetsky State Historical and Architectural Museum was established and restoration of what remained of the monastery began. In 1990 – two years after the celebration of the millennium of Russia's conversion to Christianity–the Orthodox Church regained possession of part of the monastery, and monks returned to the islands. In August 1992 the Patriarch of Moscow and All Russia Alexei II reconsecrated the Solovetsky Monastery and celebrated a mass for the reburial of the remains of the monastery's founders, Savvaty, Zosima and Herman, in the crypt. After 65 years in exile, the relics of the anchorite saints had returned from St. Petersburg to the Solovetsky Islands. That same year, the Solovetsky monastery complex was included in UNESCO's World Heritage List.

The man in the photograph was arrested on a suburban train in Leningrad Oblast because he publicly called the Bolsheviks the anti-Christ. Upon being detained he refused to give his name or sign any documents. On his charge sheet the official wrote "Unknown No 2." The man also objected to having his photograph taken. He was sentenced to five years in the camps.

Members of certain religious sects, including the Old Believers, refused to cooperate in any way with the Soviet authorities. They totally rejected Bolshevism in the belief that it was a manifestation of Satan on Earth. They would not touch any documents issued by the new authorities, including passports, and they refused to give their names. In the camps, they did not go to work despite the brutal repression of the supervisors; starved and persecuted, they were the first to die.

Charge Sheet: Unknown Citizen No 2, to be kept in custody: 1st LO [Leningrad Oblast] prison, registered and held there: UNKVD prison [three officials' signatures], the charge sheet was read out to me: refused [to sign]. I hereby sanction this arrest, Assistant Provincial Prosecutor, LOUM [Leningrad Oblast Militia] Division: [official's signature]

Prisoners on their way from
Murmansk railroad station to
the transit camp for the
Solovetsky Special Purpose
Camp, located at Kem on the
White Sea, 1927-1928.

The gate of Solovetsky transit camp. Inscribed above the gate: USSR. *Sollager* Administration ONOGPU (Administration of the Solovetsky Special Purpose Camps OGPU)], *Kemperpunkt* – short for *Kemsky peresylny punkt* (or Kem Transit Camp). Kem on the White Sea, 1927-1928.

Loading prisoners onto the *Gleb Boky*
and setting sail for the camp on the
Solovetsky Islands.
Kem, 1927-1928.

Harbor in Blagopoluchie Bay, 1920s. Arrival of a new consignment of prisoners on the Solovetsky Islands. The *Gleb Boky* and the *Klara Zetkin*, both owned by the camp, supplied Solovki with prisoners and provisions. The navigation season lasted for a few months. In the winter, when the White Sea was frozen, the Solovetsky Islands were cut off from the world.

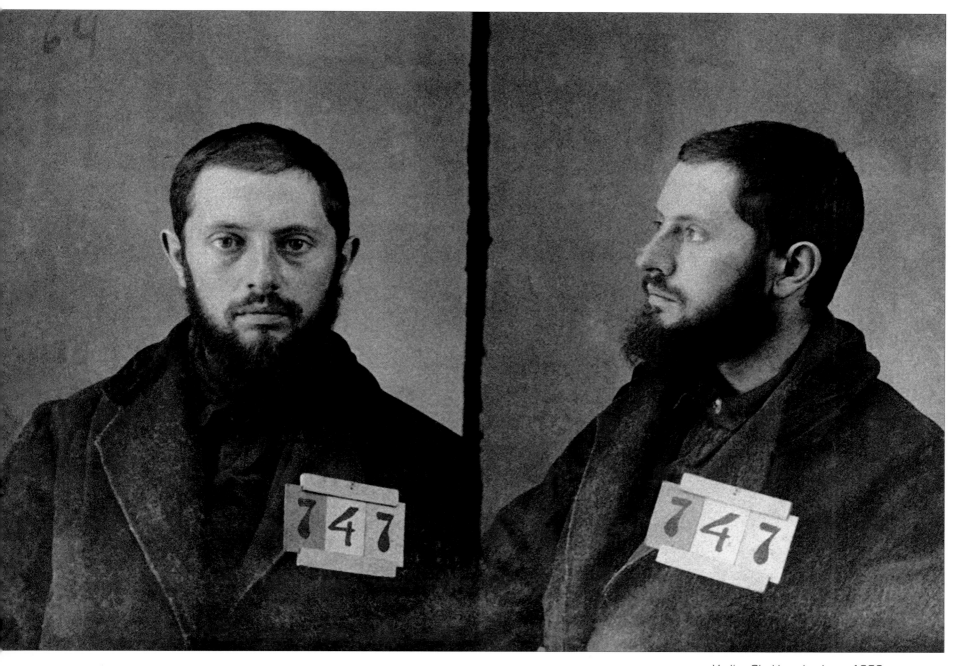

Vadim Chekhovsky, born 1902,
meteorologist and chemist. Shot
at the Solovetsky camp in 1929.

Viktor Khorodchinsky, born 1913,
poet. Arrested at the age of 15
and prisoner at the Solovetsky
camp from 1929 to 1931. After a
year's break again imprisoned at
Solovki from 1932 to 1936 and
shot in 1937.

Vadim Verbitsky, born 1897,
professional soldier, commander of a
regiment in Semion Petlura's army in
Ukraine. Shot at the Solovetsky camp
in 1929.

Vatslav Dvorzhetsky, born 1910, actor,
in the Solovetsky camp from 1929 to
1932. Spent a total of 27 years in the
camps and in exile; died in 1993 in
Nizhny Novgorod

Feliks Lubczyński, born 1886 in the province
of Volhynia. A Polish Catholic priest,
arrested in 1927, accused of anti-Soviet
propaganda, and condemned to 10 years in
the camps. Died at the Solovetsky camp on
November 17, 1931.

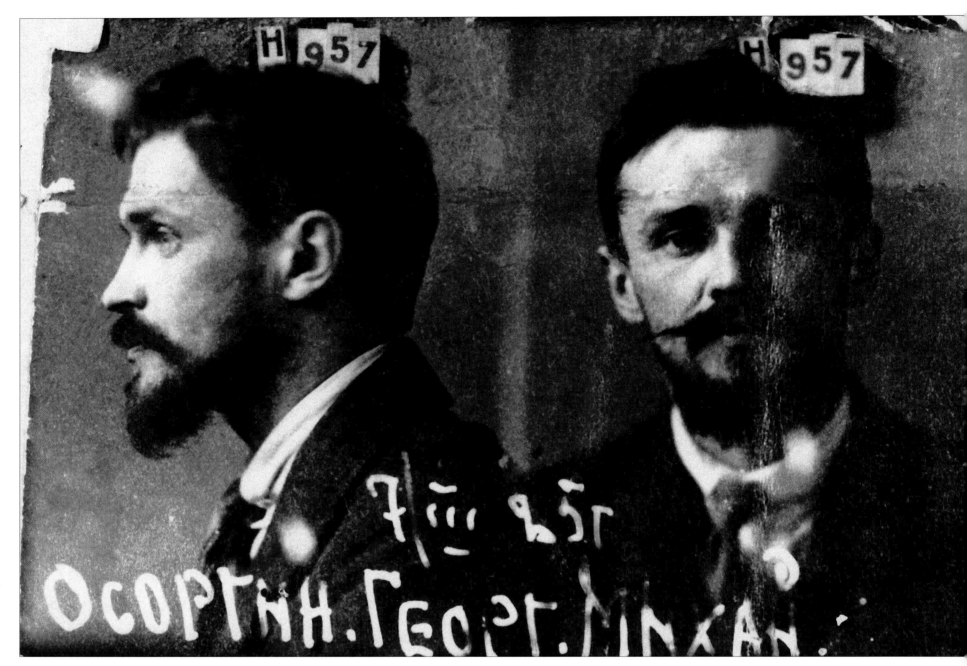

Giorgy Osorgin, born 1893, officer in
the Czarist army, prisoner at the
Solovetsky camp from 1925 and shot
there in 1929.

Evgenia Yaroslavskaia-Manron, born
1906, poet, journalist. Shot at the
Solovetsky camp in 1931.

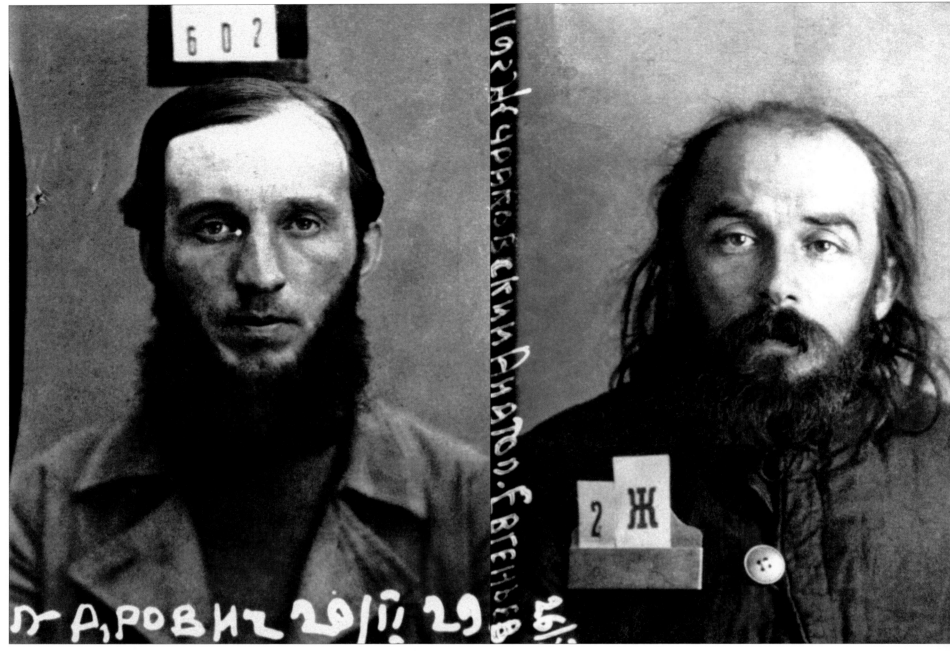

Igor Kurilko, born 1904, nobleman,
lieutenant in the Czarist army.
Condemned to five years in the camps
for "anti-Soviet propaganda." Foreman
of the transit camp at Kem, renowned
for his cruelty and sadism. He appears
in many prisoners' memoirs; Alexander
Solzhenitsyn also writes about him in
The Gulag Archipelago. He was
condemned to death and shot in 1930.

Anatoly Zhurakovsky, born 1897,
Orthodox priest, poet. Shot at the
Solovetsky camp in 1937.

Ivan Seletsky, born 1884 in Yaroslavl. A lawyer and a staff officer in the Czarist army. He was imprisoned in 1905 for revolutionary activity. From 1917 a member of the Russian Communist Party (Bolshevik), a regiment commander in the Red Army and later director of the "Red Rubber" enterprise. He was arrested in June 1924, for political provocation and for impersonating an OGPU agent. This picture was taken in custody on January 19, 1925, seven months after his arrest. Seletsky was probably beaten during the inquiry because he refused to confess to the made-up charges. The photograph was glued onto a piece of paper torn from the minutes of the interrogation, on which Ivan Seletsky had written in large letters, "I have never been an agent" and his sentence was later commuted to 10 years in the Solovetsky camp.

Priests from the Russian Orthodox Church imprisoned at the Solovetsky camp. Sitting from left to right: Father Alexei Shishkin from Novocherkassk, Archbishop Mitrofan Grinev, Archbishop Ilarion Troitsky, Metropolitan Evgeny Zhernov, Archbishop Zakharia Lobov, Father Pavel Chekhranov from Rostov-on-Don. Standing from left to right: Fathers Semion Krasnov, Iliya Pirozhenko, Alexei Trefilev, Piotr Falevich, Vladimir Volagurin.

Solovetsky camp, 1926.

Profanation of the graves of Savvaty, Zosima and Herman, founders of the
Solovetsky Monastery. Relics are objects of particular veneration in the
Orthodox Church. Among the populace it was commonly believed that the
bodies of saints did not decompose after death and imparted strength to
the believers. As part of their fight against religion, the Bolsheviks
conducted a campaign throughout Russia opening burial crypts and putting
the remains of the saints on public display. Solovetsky Monastery, 1925.

Hierarchs of the Russian Orthodox Church coming out of the chapel after holy mass. Until 1929 the priests at the Solovetsky camp could conduct Sunday services for themselves and a few prisoners who had obtained permits. The services were held in the Saint Onufry church in the monastery cemetery. This privilege was later abolished and the chapel was torn down to provide construction material for the local power station. The graveyard was also destroyed.

The camp's distribution point for postal parcels for prisoners,
1927-1928.

*Prisoners who do not receive any help from home in the form
of parcels or money, but must rely on the pitiful prison rations
are condemned to death by starvation because of permanent
malnutrition.*

From the memoirs of Ivan Zaitsev.

Camp roll call in the monastery
courtyard, 1927-1928.

Guards of the Solovetsky Special
Purpose Camp, 1932.

One of the camp's activities was fishing.
The Solovetsky camp had at its disposal
the schooner *Novye Solovki*, which fished
on behalf of an enterprise run by the
camp. Inmates worked at sea and
processed the fish. The Filomonovsky
fishing ground; first from the left is
Archbishop Ilarion Troitsky. Great
Solovetsky Island, 1925.

Building a section of the narrow-gauge railroad leading to the brickyard. Great Solovetsky Island, 1924-1925.

Mining peat deposits, Great
Solovetsky Island, 1927.

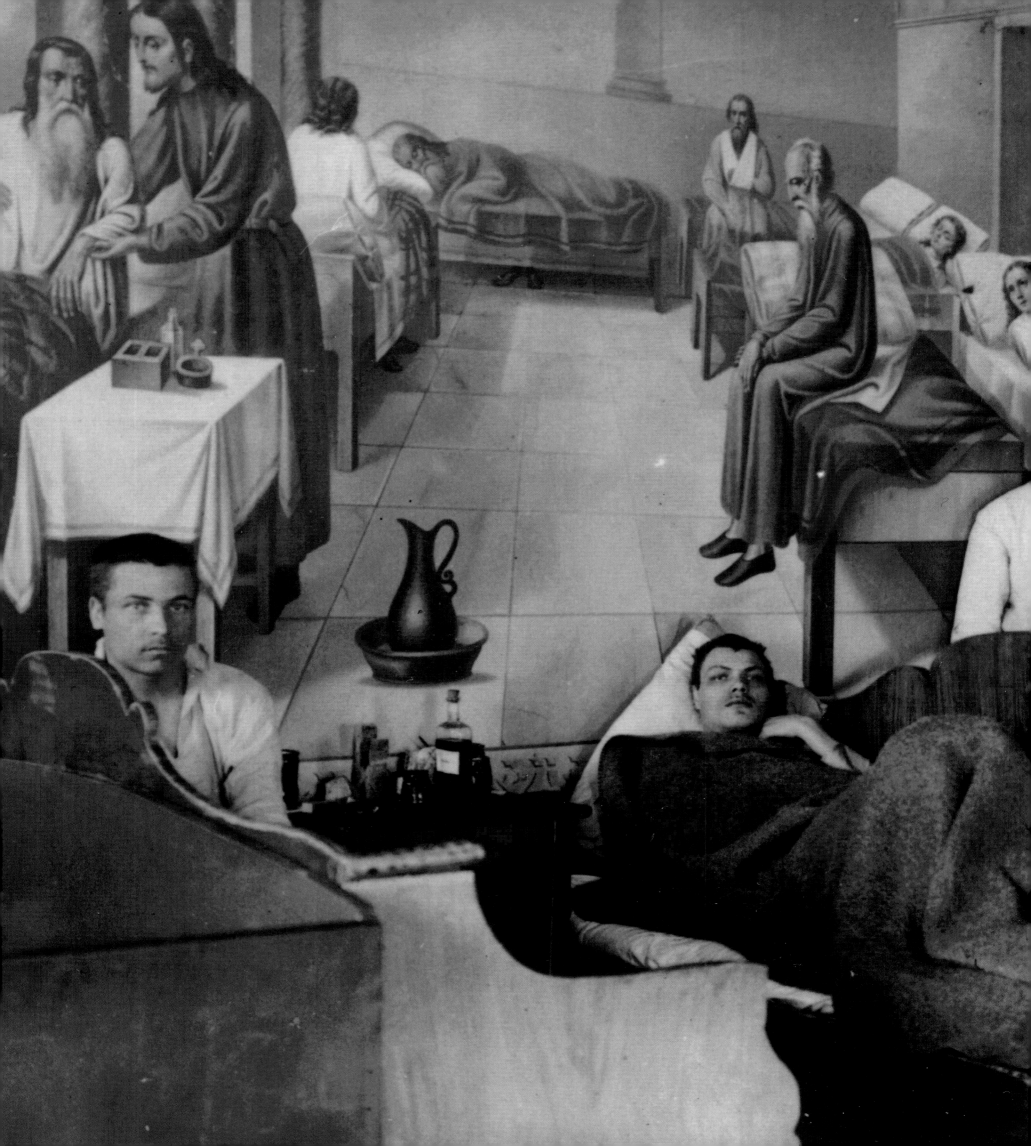

The monastery hospital converted
into the camp infirmary, 1924.

The writer Maxim Gorky visiting the Solovetsky camp, June 20-23, 1929.

Arriving at Solovki on board the *Gleb Boky*. Standing from left to right: M. Pogrebinsky, Alexandr Nogtev, director of the Solovetsky Special Purpose Camp, Gorky's daughter-in-law "Timosha" (facing away), Gorky's son Maxim Peshkov, anon.

Maxim Gorky with Gleb Boky, director of the OGPU Special Division III, which ran the labor camps in the USSR, at the sub-camp on Big Muxalma island.

Beside me sits a man who is a revolutionary Bolshevik of the old school. I know almost his entire life story and all about his work, and I would like to tell him of my respect for people of his kind, of the warm personal feelings I have for him...

Maxim Gorky in his article entitled "Solovki."

Visiting a penal isolation cell in the Church of the Ascension on Sekirnaia Mountain, renowned for its very harsh regime and the cruelty of the supervisors. Coming out of the church, Gleb Boky noted in his duty log, "During my visit I found everything in good order on Serkirnaia"; lower down Maxim Gorky added, "I would say excellent" and signed his name. Stalin was informed of this postscript in a special telegram sent from the camp to the Central Committee of the All-Union Communist Party (Bolshevik). From left to right: anon, Maxim Peshkov, Gorky's daughter-in-law "Timosha," Gleb Boky, Maxim Gorky, M. Pogrebinsky, Alexandr Nogtev, anon.

97747 НОГТЕВ Ал.Ал.ПЕТРОВ. 1892г

Alexandr Nogtev, born 1892. Following the Bolshevik Revolution of 1917, he carried out missions in the north of Russia on Lenin's orders, and worked for the Cheka-OGPU from 1921 on. He was organizer and director of the Northern Concentration Camps in the Arkhangelsk region. In 1923-1924 he became the first director of the Solovetsky Special Purpose Camp, then the director of the OGPU Special Division Department III, which ran the camps. In 1929-1930 he was again director of the Solovetsky camp. He personally signed proposals addressed to the OGPU's governing body to issue death sentences for prisoners without trial. In 1932 he was discharged from the security organs and worked in Moscow at the Glavdrov Association in charge of forestry. Arrested in 1938, he was accused of counter-revolutionary activity and terrorism. Sentenced to 15 years in the camps, he served his time in Krasnoiarsk Krai. He was released after seven years under the terms of the 1945 amnesty. He died in Moscow in 1947.

Picture of Alexandr Nogtev taken at Lubianka prison. Moscow, September 1938.

Alexandr Nogtev in the camp in April 1944;
this picture was sent to his wife Margarita.

Alexandr Nogtev, 1918.

On the back of the picture is written:

The days go by,
the nights go by,
the summer is over,
yellow leaves are rustling.
My eyes are asleep,
my thoughts and heart are asleep...
Everything is asleep...
And I don't know if I'm alive
or just living out the years
or just roaming the earth
Neither in tears
nor in laughter.

April 12, 1944

SOLOVKI
Historical note

The Solovetsky Special Purpose Camp – known by its Russian acronym SLON, from *Solovetsky Lager Osobovogo Naznachenia* – was established in 1923 in a monastery on the Solovetsky Islands in the White Sea and was the embryo of the Gulag camp system in the USSR. At the time of its foundation, there were about 700 concentration camps, penal colonies and "houses of corrective labor" in Soviet Russia, but they were subordinate to various organs of authority and their administration was decentralized. The Solovetsky camp was the first to be directly under the control of the OGPU, which centralized and expanded the camp system. It was completed in 1930 with the establishment of the Chief Administration of Corrective Labor, shortened to Chief Camp Administration – in Russian, *Glavnoye Upravlenie Lagerey*, or GULAG.

At the Solovetsky camps, the prisoners did the following work:
• worked in forestry and mined peat deposits
• fished for freshwater and marine fish
• slaughtered sea mammals and extracted blubber
• worked in the brickyards, shipyard, lime works, machine shops, tailor, pottery and shoe repair workshops
• farmed and raised fur-bearing animals
• researched the adaptation of plants to the northern climate, and the industrial uses of seaweeds.

In the SLON sub-camps on the mainland the prisoners did the following work:
• worked in forestry
• constructed roads in Karelia, including four strategic routes leading to the Finnish border: Kem-Ukhta, Loukhi-Kiestinga, Vostochnaia-Guba-Karmasielga, and Parandovo-Tishkozero
• started preparations for the construction of the northern section of the White Sea Canal
• loaded and unloaded trains for the Murmansk railroad.

Between 1923 and 1929 no fewer than 840,000 inmates passed through the Solovetsky camps. Data published on the mortality rate among prisoners are incomplete; for example, in 1926-1927, 728 prisoners died at Solovki in a twelve month period, while between 1929 and 1930, 979 people died in the Golgotha sub-camp alone in an eight-month period. The number of victims of the Solovetsky camps has not yet been established, but it is estimated that about 15,000 people died there.

1918

Corn at the Solovetsky Monastery is requisitioned by a Red Army unit from Arkhangelsk. The RSFSR Council of People's Commissars issues a decree depriving the Russian Orthodox Church of its legal status; Church property now belongs to the people.

1919

The authorities open 39 tombs of Russian Orthodox saints and put the remains on public display as part of their campaign against religion. The relics of Saint Sergei Randonezhsky, worshipped throughout Russia, are desecrated at the Troitsky Monastery near Moscow.

1920

On May 25, all the monastery's buildings and property are seized by the Arkhangelsk Executive Committee of the Russian Communist Party (Bolshevik). All valuables are requisitioned. The Solovki sovkhoz is established; its full name is the Soviet Farm Administration on the Solovetsky Islands. The Compulsory Labor Camp for Prisoners of War is opened for about 300 soldiers who had fought for the White Army in the Civil War.
Political Commissar S. A. Abakumov is appointed commander of the Solovetsky Islands. In Russia mass arrests of the Orthodox clergy and further desecration of holy relics take place.

1922

The Patriarch of Moscow and All Russia, Tikhon (born Vasily Belavin) is arrested (he died in exile in 1925). The Metropolitan of Petrograd, Veniamin (born Vasily Kazansky) is arrested, condemned to death and shot. The remains of Saint Alexander Nevsky are desecrated in Petrograd.

1923

In September, the number of prisoners at Solovki is 3,049.
Alexandr Nogtev is appointed head of the Solovetsky camp.
The manager of the Solovki sovkhoz deliberately sets fire to the Solovetsky Monastery. Inmates from the OGPU's Northern Concentration Camps are transferred from Arkhangelsk, Kholmogory and Petrominsk to the Solovetsky Islands.
On October 13, the Solovetsky Special Purpose Camp, SLON, is established by a resolution of the USSR Council of People's Commissars. Camp farming, fishing, forestry and other economic activities are now exempt from taxes and local dues.

Minutes of the meeting of the USSR Council of People's Commissars, October 13, 1923

The Council of People's Commissars resolves:

1. To establish the Solovetsky Special Purpose Compulsory Labor Camp and two transit and distribution points at Arkhangelsk and Kem.
2. To put the OGPU in charge of establishing and managing the camp and transit and distribution points mentioned in point 1.
3. To transfer to the OGPU all the possessions, buildings, livestock inventory (dead and alive) that formerly belonged to Solovetsky Monastery, and also to the Petrominsk camp and the Arkhangelsk transit and distribution point.

Deputy Chairman of the Council of People's Commissars Rykov
Executive Secretary of the Council of People's Commissars Gorbunov

Further large-scale persecution of the Russian Orthodox Church follows. (In 1922-1923 2,700 Orthodox priests, 3,400 nuns and 2,000 monks were killed. Almost the entire episcopate was imprisoned in the camps or sentenced to exile.)

1924

The average number of prisoners is 4,100.
On March 3, the SLON Statute is ratified by the OGPU's governing body.

1925

The average number of prisoners is 6,800.
The tombs of Saints Zosima, Savvaty and Herman are opened and their remains are publicly displayed in the camp (they were later sent to the Museum of Atheism in Kazan Cathedral, Leningrad).

1926

The average number of prisoners is 9,300.
A letter is sent to the USSR government signed by 23 archbishops and bishops imprisoned in the Solovetsky camp. They asked for the freedom to operate religious communities, religious liberties and the rights to preach as guaranteed by the Soviet Constitution. An appeal is made to stop the persecution of the Russian Orthodox Church.
SLON opens branches on the mainland, in Karelia, on the Kola Peninsula and in the Urals.

1927

The average number of prisoners is 12,700.
A propaganda film entitled *Solovki* is made by a Sovkino film crew, in which the Solovetsky camp is presented as a place where criminals are "re-socialized" (the filming is completed the next year).

Nationality profile of prisoners at the Solovetsky camp on October 1, 1927:

Russian:	9,364	German:	65	Chinese:	24	French:	8
Jewish:	739	Uzbek:	63	Kalmyk:	23	Buryat:	5
Belarussian:	592	Finnish:	62	Gypsy:	22	Karaimov:	5
Polish:	353	Ossetian:	59	Greek:	20	Dagestani:	4
Ukrainian:	229	Lithuanian:	58	Turkish:	14	Kabardin:	4
Turkmen:	198	Karelian:	48	Czech:	13	Kyrgyz:	4
Tatar:	184	Hungarian:	40	Moldavian:	8	Servian:	3
Georgian:	184	Iranian:	39	Sart:	8	Italian:	2
Estonian:	113	Chuvash:	32	Gorets:	7	Albanian:	1
Armenian:	108	Chechen:	29	Romanian:	7	Zyrian:	1
Latvian:	91	Lezgian:	28	Tavlin:	7	Korean:	1
Circassian:	89	Ingush:	26	Afghan:	8	Cheremish:	1

Total : 12,896

1928

The number of prisoners on April 1 is 13,366.
Fiodor Eikhmans is appointed head of the Solovetsky Special Purpose Camp.

1929

The average number of prisoners is 21,900.
Alexandr Nogtev is re-appointed head of the Solovetsky Special Purpose Camp.
On June 20-23, Maxim Gorky visits the Solovetsky Islands. Gorky's article entitled "Solovki" is published in the Soviet and foreign press. In it he confirms his support for the policy of "education through work" conducted in the OGPU's camps.
There is a typhoid epidemic in the camp, a lack of medicine and medical staff. Large numbers of prisoners die and are buried in communal graves.
On October 1, the Solovetsky camp becomes self-financing.

1930

The average number of prisoners is 65,000.
A. A. Ivanchenko is appointed head of the Solovetsky camp.
On April 25, the OGPU's ULAG Camp Administration is instituted by a resolution of the USSR Council of People's Commissars dated April 7, 1930 (a few months later the name was changed to Chief Camp Administration, *Glavnoye Upravlenie Lagerei*, or GULAG).
The OGPU's special investigative commission arrives from Moscow to research abuses at the camp. About 60 people are shot, mainly criminals serving as camp supervisors and a few administrative officials charged with the rape, torture and murder of prisoners. (The institution of OGPU's investigative commission was probably the result of Maxim Gorky's visit the year before. According to Dmitry Likhachev, historian of literature and prisoner at Solovki, the writer prevailed upon the authorities to look into the situation at the camp.)

1931

The number of prisoners on 1 January is 71,800.

E. I. Sienkiewicz is appointed head of the Solovetsky camp.

Large numbers of prisoners are transferred from Solovki to the construction site at the White Sea Canal.

1932

The average number of prisoners is 15,130.

1933

The average number of prisoners is 19,280.

On December 4, SLON is converted into the Solovetsky Sub-Camp for the White Sea-Baltic Corrective Labor Camp, Belbaltlag.

Buchband is appointed head of the Solovetsky sub-camp, followed by Evlev (first names not known).

1936

There is no data on the number of prisoners.

On November 28, the Solovetsky Sub-Camp Belbaltlag is converted into the Solovetsky Special Purpose Prison (*Solovetskaia Tiurma Osobovogo Naznachenya*, acronym STON) subordinate to the NKVD's Chief Administration of State Security.

1937-1938

There is no data on the number of prisoners.

At least 1,825 prisoners at Solovki are shot during the Great Purge.

1939

The number of prisoners is 4,500.

On November 2, the Solovetsky Special Purpose Prison, STON, is closed down.

1940-1973

A naval base is established. The Solovetsky Monastery undergoes further destruction. A settlement develops on Great Solovetsky Island.

1974

The Solovetsky State Historical and Architectural Museum and Nature Reserve is founded, and monastery restoration begins.

1990

Some of the monastery buildings are returned to the Russian Orthodox Church, and monks return to Solovki. A permanent exhibition, "The Solovetsky Special Purpose Camps, 1923-1939", is opened, organized by the Memorial Society and the Solovetsky Museum.

1992

Religious ceremonies are held with the participation of Patriarch of Moscow and All Russia Alexei II to celebrate the return from Saint Petersburg to Solovki of the remains of Saints Savvaty, Zosima and Herman, the 15th-century founders of the monastery.

The naval base on the Solovetsky Islands is closed.

The Solovetsky Monastery complex is included in UNESCO's World Heritage List.

1993

Alexander Solzhenitsyn, author of *The Gulag Archipelago*, provides funding for a motor yacht, *Monastyrsky*, for the Solovetsky Monastery, which is used for communication with the mainland.

Sources :

1. Yury Brodsky, *Solovki. Dvadsat let osobovogo naznachenya* ["Solovki. Twenty years of special purpose"], published by *Rossyskaia Politicheskaia Entsiklopedia*, Moscow 2002.

2. Ivan Chukhin, *Kanaloarmeitsy, Istoria stroitelstva Belomorkanala* ["The Canal Army, a history of the construction of the White Sea Canal"], published by "Karelia", Petrozavodsk 1990.

3. Sergei Krivenko, "OGPU's Solovetsky Corrective Labor Camp" ["The Prison Camps. An Encyclopedic Guide"], issued by the Memorial Center for Research, Information and Dissemination (NIPC) in Moscow, jointly edited by Nikita Okhotin and Arseny Roginsky.

4. Piotr Mitzner, *Rosja bez Cerkwi* ["Russia without the Church"], in the Polish historical quarterly *Karta*, No 15, Warsaw 1995.

5. Mikhail Rozanov, *Solovetsky kontslager v monastyre 1922-1939* ["The Solovetsky concentration camp in a monastery 1922-1939"], published by the author, 1979.

6. V. Skopin, *Na Solovetskich Ostrovakh* ["On the Solovetsky Islands"], published in *Isskustvo*, Moscow 1991.

7. Quotes from *Solovki. Dvadsat let osobovogo naznacheniya* ["Solovki. Twenty years of special purpose"] by Yury Brodsky. Moscow. *Rosly Skaya Politicheskaya Enciklopedia 2002*.

SOLOVKI DOCUMENTS

Top secret.
Director of Leningrad Oblast UNKVD
Commissar for State Security comrade Zakovsky
re: my order No. 00447

I hereby order:

1. Starting on August 25 and finishing within two months, an operation to repress the most active counter-revolutionary elements held in the GUGB (Chief Administration of State Security) prisons, sentenced for activities involving spying, sabotage, terrorism, insurgency and banditry, and also condemned members of anti-Soviet parties (Trotskyites, Social Revolutionaries, Georgian Mensheviks, Dashnaks, Ittkhatists, Mussavatists etc.) and all other counter-revolutionaries conducting anti-Soviet activity in GUGB prisons ...

2. All the above-mentioned groups, following examination of their cases by the NKVD Troika, are to be shot.

3. The repression of 1,200 people from Solovetsky prison is confirmed for you...

Narkom (People's Commissariat) for Internal Affairs of the USSR
Commissar General for State Security Yezhov

October 16, 1937
Top secret. For your eyes only.
Deputy Director of Arkhangelsk Administration, Leningrad Oblast NKVD
Captain of State Security comrade Matveev.

Order No. 189852
You are hereby ordered that those condemned by the Special Troika of the Leningrad Oblast NKVD, in accordance with the attached copies of Troika Protocols Nos 81, 82, 83, 84 and 85, dated 9, 10 and 14 October of this year – 1,116 people in total, held at the GUGB (Chief Administration of State Security) of the NKVD of the USSR Solovetsky Prison are TO BE SHOT.
For this purpose you are to leave immediately for Kem. Contact the director of the GUGB Solovetsky Prison, Senior Major of State Security comrade Apetier. He has already received orders to hand over the prisoners and to carry out the sentence according to instructions that you have personally received.

Director of Administration, Leningrad Oblast NKVD
Commissar for State Security Grade III Zakovsky.
Director of III Division of State Security Administration
Senior Lieutenant Yegorov.

Deputy Director of Administration, Leningrad Oblast NKVD
Senior Major of State Security comrade Garin
Report.

I report that in accordance with Order No. 189852, dated October 16, 1937, issued by Director of Administration, Leningrad Oblast NKVD, Commissar for State Security 1st Rank comrade Zakovsky dated October 16, 1937, No. 189852, I have carried out the sentence concerning those condemned to death in accordance with protocols Nos 81, 82, 83, 84 and 85 – 1,116 people in total.

Deputy Director of Arkhangelsk Administration, Leningrad Oblast NKVD
Captain of State Security Matveev.

Top secret. For your eyes only.
Leningrad Oblast UNKVD Commander
Senior Lieutenant of State Security comrade Polikarpov

Order No. 193920
You are hereby ordered that those condemned by the Special Troika of the Leningrad Oblast NKVD, in accordance with the attached copies of Troika Protocols Nos 134, 198 and 199, dated November 10 and 25 of this year, as well as those who have arrived from GUGB of the NKVD of the USSR Solovetsky Special Purpose Prison are TO BE SHOT...

Director of Administration, Leningrad Oblast NKVD
Commissar for State Security Grade III Zakovsky.
Director of III Division of State Security Administration
Senior Lieutenant Egorov.
December 7, 1937

Sources :
Based on *Solovki. Dvadsat let osobovogo naznacheniya* ["Solovki. Twenty years of special purpose"] by Yury Brodsky.

As soon as we went on board we were separated: women fore and men aft. Soon a shrill noise rose from the women's part of the ship – an orgy had begun. The Cheka men did not immediately resort to rape, as the guards in the train had done. First they gave the women some food and a lot of vodka, and when they were drunk, the men shared the women among themselves. We sat aft with our heads lowered.

From the memoirs of Emelian Solovev

The arrival of new consignments of prisoners was a terrifying event almost impossible to describe. The prisoners were humiliated, showered in the worst abuse and beaten with wooden sticks; in summer they were stripped naked and exposed to the mosquitoes, made to stand still …

As they crossed the bridge, the supervisors pointed at one prisoner and shouted, "Dolphin!" That prisoner had to jump into the water. If he didn't, he'd be beaten and forcibly thrown in.

For the smallest infringement of the rules, prisoners were beaten and put in the "kibitki" – isolation cells made from planks knocked together, with no heating, where they were kept until their extremities were frostbitten. To torture the prisoners special isolation cells were also made, one meter high, with the ceiling, floor and walls studded with sharp wooden nails. Prisoners who ended up in there often couldn't withstand the torment and died.

From the documents of the OGPU Special Investigative Commission.

The treatment meted out to prisoners by the camp guards was severe, bordering on sadism. Typical punishments included beatings with a club, being doused in water in freezing weather, being dropped into an ice hole, or being kept out in the frost for several hours.

From Polish intelligence documents.

Hardest of all were the sub-camps, where they worked in the forest, felling trees. In the winter the prisoners worked for 10 hours there. Quite often they were forced to work half-dressed, in sub-zero temperatures. They worked far beyond their capacity. Their feet and hands became frostbitten. There were cases of freezing to death. The brigades that fulfill the norms were often forced to work until late at night. They came back to the barracks, slept three or four hours, and did not have time to dry out their clothes before they were forced to go out to work again.

In these sub-camps people literally wasted away, as they say at SLON, they were brought to the camp seriously ill, emaciated, sometimes unable to walk by themselves. A strong, healthy man quickly turned into a skeleton, into a shadow. Death from exhaustion was constant and omnipresent.

There were a lot of so-called "self-cutters" – people who deliberately cut off their own fingers and toes with axes in order to get out of those sub-camps.

From the testimony of prisoner Igor Kurilko, brigade commander (foreman) at the Kem transit camp, to the OGPU Special Investigative Commission

To the Director of the Medical Division from Doctor Lidia Volskaia
Report. I hereby inform you, that December 24, 1928, I examined the group of prisoners who had arrived from the Krasnaia Gorka and Paranovo sub-camps, and found that 75 percent of them had frostbitten extremities.

The 30th work brigade was housed in the Cathedral of the Holy Trinity, and the toilet was deliberately installed on the site of the altar.

From the memoirs of Dmitry Likhachev

Quotes based on *Solovki. Dvadsat let osobovogo naznachenya* ["Solovki. Twenty years of special purpose"] by Yuri Brodsky.

SOLOVKI
M e m o r i e s

Church of the Crucifixion in the Golgotha
Hermitage on Anzer Island where prisoners
suffering from infectious diseases, such
as consumption, typhoid and dysentery,
were held.

GOLGOTHA

The second convict work brigade of the Anzer sub-camp, Solovetsky Special Purpose Camp Department IV, located at Golgotha Hermitage on Anzer Island.

What I saw on arriving at the Golgotha sub-camp was shocking. The cramped and crowded rooms, had such a musty stench that simply remaining in them felt lethal. Despite the freezing cold, most of the people were completely undressed, naked in the full sense of the word. The rest wore pitiful rags. Emaciated people, skeletons wrapped in skin, shaking, ran naked out of the church to a hole in the ice to scoop out water with a tin can. There were cases when they died on the way.

From the testimony of prisoner S. P. Rakht to the
OGPU Special Investigative Commission

Through the window I saw naked people being driven out of the fourth barrack in minus 20 degrees Celsius down to the lake, where there was a bath house, and then back up the hill. After such an episode some of them ended up in the hospital. Up to 20 people died each day. I remember a terrible image, when from the Kaporskaia sub-camp, three kilometers away, on a frosty day in February, they drove naked people to Golgotha and into the fourth barrack. In Barracks No. 4 the temperature was middling, and the other prisoners called its inhabitants, who didn't have any clothes, "the arctic foxes". To relieve themselves they went outside completely naked. Often as a punishment they were made to stand outside in the frost, where they cried in the piercing wind, screamed and begged to be let back inside the barrack.

From the testimony of prisoner Emanuil Krutovy

I know of a case when prisoners Mastiugin and Kharitonov were beaten by Belov (gang commander) and Bakko (assistant gang commander). Mastiugin and Kharitonov were beaten unconscious. On the orders of Belov and Bakko, I got a piece of cord, stripped the prisoners to their underwear, tied their arms behind their backs above the elbows, then tied one leg to their hands by bending it back. This position caused severe pain. When I untied the prisoner he could not move his arms for a long time. Tied up like this, the prisoners were put in the bell tower, where there was snow on the ground and the wind was blowing from all directions. Bakko said they were being put there "to cool down." I was just fulfilling my duties as supervisor of the isolation cell...

From the testimony of prisoner Krylov

The belfry of Golgotha Hermitage was used as an isolation cell where prisoners were left tied up for many hours in the freezing cold. In the background is the Church of the Crucifixion.

The Golgotha Hermitage on Anzer Island.

"On May 28, 1930, I was presented with the prisoner Yulis Isaak and told that he had been shut up undressed in winter in the bell tower, where he spent 48 hours. During this time he was taken six times to a heated room where he was beaten."

From the statements of a doctor

At the foot of Golgotha Hill was a small chapel where about 200 prisoners lived on two levels of wooden bunks. This chapel was called the "bloody cook-shop," as Golgotha's commander, P. P. Belov, used to say laughing. Belov used to amuse himself by unexpectedly dragging a prisoner (by the hair) down from the upper level and banging his head against the floor. On May 10, 1930, on Belov's orders, "perches" were introduced in the chapel at Golgotha. The prisoner was forced to sit without moving for 18 hours a day and given something to eat once every three days. There were two kinds of "perch." The first sort was regarded as easier, when the prisoner's legs touched the floor. The other kind was when his legs hung in the air and his extremities swelled up.

From an indictment by the OGPU Special Investigative Commission

The graveyard at the Golgotha sub-camp consists of seven large and nine small graves. When one large grave was opened, it was found to be full of corpses to a height of a quarter of an arshin [about 20 centimeters] from ground surface. During the investigation it was established that in the winter of 1929-1930 the large graves, which could hold up to 800 corpses, were filled up and left open. These graves were situated in a visible spot, on a slope opposite the main buildings where the prisoners were housed.

From an indictment by the OGPU Special Investigative Commission

The whole system of beating and abusing the prisoners really was a system, not just individual cases. The hired bosses knew all about it and encouraged it by never taking any action to stop it...We knew perfectly well that the same thing, worse even, was happening at Solovki, at Sekirts, at all the sub-camps. Potomkin, and the other heads like him, conformed to the general situation, the general state of affairs, which became a system...

From the testimony of defendant Igor Kurilko, brigade commander (foreman) at the Kem transit camp

The OGPU Special Investigative Commission came from Moscow to the Solovetsky Islands in 1930 to investigate abuses committed by camp staff. The investigation did not include the heads of the camp, only prisoners serving as camp foremen and some officials from the camp administration.

Quotes from Yury Brodsky, *Solovki, Dvadtsat' let ossobogo naznachenia (Solovki. Twenty Years of Special Purpose).* Moscow. Rossiiskaia Politicheskaia Entsyklopedia, 2002.

Orthodox monks returned to the
monastery on the Solovetsky
Islands in 1990.

Procession of the Feast of St. Savvaty,
the founder of the Sovoletsky Monastery.

After the war, a settlement was
established near the monastery for the
families of sailors serving in the naval
unit posted on the Solovetsky Islands.
Later people came to live here from
various parts of the Soviet Union.

Yuri Kritsky, graduate of the Leningrad Historical Institute and member of the Soviet Communist Party. He worked as an archivist in Tashkent, on Vaalam Island and, for many years, at the Solovetsky State Historical and Architectural Museum. After the dissolution of the Soviet Communist Party, he joined the newly formed Russian Communist Party. In the 1970s he entirely lost his hearing due to illness. He lived alone in the Solovki village. He died in an Arkhangelsk home for the aged in the mid 1990s.

Mikhail Galinsky, graduate of the St. Petersburg Communications
Institute, where he had refused to join the Komsomol (Communist
Youth League). In 1982 he moved to the Solovetsky Islands, where he
worked on the monastery restoration, in a bar and at a smithy as
laboratory assistant, stoker, teacher, museum guard and tour guide.
In 1990 he helped transport a boulder from the Solovetsky Islands to
Moscow for a monument to the victims of Soviet communism. During
the 1992 putsch, he copied down Boris Yeltsin's edicts from the
radio and hung them up around the Solovetsky settlement. He now
repairs watches, refrigerators and radio sets. He also does voluntary
work for the elderly.

Piotr Deisan graduated with a degree in journalism from Moscow
University, served in the navy on submarines, and was a member of
the Soviet Communist Party. In the early 1980s he returned his
party membership card, for which he was persecuted and denied
work. He found a job on the local newspaper in Arkhangelsk. In
1990 he came to the Solovetsky Islands to attend a symposium on
"The Destalinization of Consciousness" and stayed for good. In
1993 he was admitted to novitiate at the Solovetsky Monastery.
Following conflict with the monks he left the monastery because he
refused to give up his dog, which he had brought up from a puppy.
He then moved to the uninhabited Zaiatskaia Island, where, as a
guard at the Solovetsky Museum, he took care of the stone
labyrinths – and a chapel founded by Peter the Great in 1702.

Vladimir Shaposhnikov, curator of icons at the Solovetsky State
Historical and Architectural Museum. He came to Solovki from
Sevastopol in 1975, at the age of 21. He received his degree as a
first-class curator of icons from the Center for the Restoration of
Antiquities in Moscow. For 18 years he has been involved in the
restoration of the Solovetsky Museum's icon collection. The icons
were brought here from churches on the White Sea coast and the
Karelian Republic. As a result of his efforts, many icons were saved
from ruin or looting.

Cecilia Melnikova in front of the ruins of the Savvatievsky
Hermitage at Solovki, where as a child she was imprisoned
with her parents. Her father, Moisei Babin, a Social Democrat,
was arrested in 1924 and sent to Solovki with his wife Daria
Tseltin and their 18-month-old daughter. Later the entire family
was deported to Perm. Her mother died in exile. Her father
was shot in 1937. Cecilia was brought up by her father's sister
in Moscow. Her mother's brothers were also at Solovki –
Mikhail, a member of the Social Revolutionary party, and
Semion, a Social Democrat. Both were shot in 1937. Mikhail's
wife, Lizaveta Bauer, died at Solovki in 1925, shot by the
guards during a protest by Social Revolutionaries and Social
Democrats fighting for the rights of political prisoners.

Vladimir Chashei, born 1910 in Riga, graduated from the Lomonosov Institute of Mechanics in Moscow. Arrested in 1934 and sentenced to five years in the camps for "anti-Soviet propaganda." In the Solovetsky camp he did general labor and worked in the machine shops. He was released in 1939. During the war he served in the Soviet Partisan Army and was imprisoned at the Nazi Stutthof concentration camp between 1943 and 1945. He was a witness at the Nuremberg trials. After the war he settled in Belarus and worked as an engineer. Now retired. Rehabilitated in 1955.

Viktor Vasiliev, born 1916 in Moscow. Had
higher education and worked as an
electrical technician for the railroads.
Arrested in 1932 and sentenced to 10
years in the camps. At Solovki he worked in
the power station and at the shipyard. From
1937 he worked as a prisoner on oil
extraction in the Karelian Republic. He was
released in 1942, re-arrested in 1950 and
sentenced to life exile in Karaganda,
Kazakhstan. He was rehabilitated in 1956.
He is the author of a collection of poems
written in the camps.

"On a cold and distant sea
there are some islands
an endless battle is fought for them
a dispute between god and the devil
but the fur flies
from such as I"

Viktor Vasiliev

Teimur Kazhiev, painter, born 1936 in the Solovetsky camp on Anzer Island. His mother, Anna Brilliantova, a prisoner at Solovki, was shot in 1937. Eighteen-month-old Teimur Kazhiev was taken from the camp to an orphanage, where three years later his grandfather retrieved him. He was then brought up by his mother's family. Meanwhile, his father, Kerim Kazhiev, was serving a 10-year sentence in the camp. Teimur Kazhiev lives in the Moscow suburbs, and is a professional painter of traditional Russian lacquer miniatures.

Nadezhda Vasilian on the return journey from the Solovetsky Islands. She is the daughter of Vladimir Rokhinson, a prisoner at the Solovetsky camp who was shot in 1937.

A mass in the Church of the Ascension on Sekirnaia Mountain to say prayers for victims of the Solovetsky camp, attended by former prisoners and relatives of those murdered.

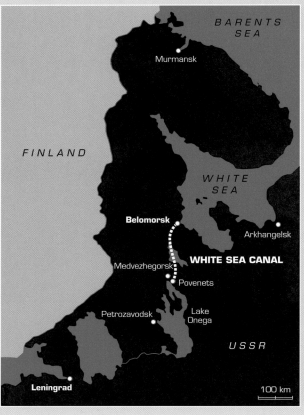

BARENTS
SEA

Murmansk

FINLAND

WHITE
SEA

Belomorsk

Arkhangelsk

WHITE SEA CANAL

Medvezhegorsk

Povenets

Petrozavodsk

Lake
Onega

USSR

Leningrad

100 km

THE WHITE SEA CANAL

THE WHITE SEA CANAL
1931-1933

In May 1933 the steamship *Anokhin* sailed from Povenets on Lake Onega to Belomorsk on the White Sea, with Joseph Stalin on board. He was there to officially open the Joseph Stalin White Sea-Baltic Canal. But the *Anokhin* was not the first ship to follow that route in history. Two hundred and thirty years earlier, in 1702, two of Peter the Great's sailing frigates, the *Courier* and the *Holy Ghost*, had made the same journey, but in the opposite direction.

During the Great Northern War against the Swedes, Peter the Great personally commanded the Russian fleet on the White Sea. On August 6, 1702, the emperor wrote from Arkhangelsk to Admiral Fiodor Apraksin, "We and our regiments are waiting only for the wind, and as soon as we get it, we shall set sail for Niukhta, and then shall travel by an overland route to Lake Onega." The Admiral must have been surprised when he read the Czar's message, because there was no "overland route" across the marshes and forests of Karelia linking the White Sea and Lake Onega. But Peter, not without good reason later named the Great, had ordered one to be built. This would require hacking out a road with axes, 180 kilometers long and over six meters wide, digging up tree roots, shifting erratic blocks, leveling the ground surface, hardening the marshes with fascines, building bridges over rivers and crossings over lakes. Thousands of serfs were recruited to do the work, and realized the emperor's vision in a record 60 days. The chroniclers describe how the frigates *Courier* and *Holy Ghost* were placed on massive sleds and pulled by teams of 100 horses each, with logs placed under the sled runners. Ten days later, the military expedition including two ships, 4,000 soldiers, the Czar and his son Alexei, reached Povenets on Lake Onega. From there the ships sailed across to Lake Ladoga. Using the tactic of surprise, Peter captured the Swedish fortress of Nöteburg, which guarded access to the Neva River. In the following year, he reached the Baltic and founded St. Petersburg – the future capital of Russia. The Czar's expedition from the White Sea to the Baltic entered the history books as "The Monarch's Way."

We still do not know exactly what inspired Stalin when, in the words of Alexander Solzhenitsyn, "while gazing at the map of northern Russia, he marked out the White Sea Canal with his pipe stem." The construction of the White Sea Canal was not envisaged in the first Five-Year Plan. So Stalin's decision to build it took everyone by surprise. He must have been convinced that the canal would have strategic and economic importance. In reality, its construction proved unnecessary. Perhaps Stalin simply wanted to associate himself with the glory of Peter the Great. Reflecting the emperor's achievement, a canal would link two seas, and he would be its namesake – and the means of implementing the project was also similar to the Czar's. Even some 80,000 prisoners from the Gulag were rounded up for slave labor: men, women, adolescents and old people. The builders had only the most primitive tools at their disposal: spades, pickaxes and hatchets. Wooden wheelbarrows were made on site, and the wheels for them were cast in improvised forges. There was no machinery. Primitive cranes were constructed out of wood, as well as pile drivers to hammer pillars into the ground, driven only by the prisoners' muscle power. Apart from explosives, which were used to split rocks, the means of carrying out "the great construction project" were practically mediaeval.

Joseph Stalin ordered the White Sea Canal to be built quickly and cheaply. It was to be made from stone, earth and wood, with minimal use of steel and cement, which in those days were expensive and in short supply. Engineers were brought from labor camps and "houses of correction" to the OGPU's Special Construction Office at the Lubianka in Moscow and told to design the project at lightning speed. It was one of the first so-called *sharashki* – Gulag camps where imprisoned specialists worked.

The White Sea Canal was one of communism's first "great construction projects" built by prison laborers. To support it the propaganda machine was cranked up to an unprecedented scale, under the slogan of *perekovka*, or "the reforging" of criminals into conscious citizens of socialist society. The slave labor of people condemned for crimes they had not committed was presented as the new, humanitarian penal policy of "the fatherland of the world proletariat." Propaganda was the domain of the Department of Culture and Education, which was responsible for a newspaper, *Perekovka*, a radio news bulletin issued over camp loudspeakers, wall newspapers (sheets put on bulletin boards), prisoner brigades that traveled up and down the canal route giving propaganda performances, and brass bands that played along to the work. "Socialist competitions" were organized between prison brigades and ceremonies were held to present the red banner of labor to shock-workers (laborers exceeding quotas). Selected prisoners spoke at public meetings about the "change in awareness that took place in them due to intensive labor on behalf of socialism."

On Stalin's orders some 120 Soviet writers and journalists were taken to the building site. In a propaganda book entitled *The Stalin White Sea-Baltic Canal* published in 1934, 36 leading Soviet writers, including Demian Bedny, Bruno Jasieński, Valentin Kataev, Viktor Shklovsky, Alexei Tolstoi and Mikhail Zoshchenko, enthusiastically described "the great construction project."

On the book's board of editors, alongside literati such as Maxim Gorky and Leopold Auerbach, as if among equals, sat the Chekist Semion Firin, head of Belbaltlag (the White Sea-Baltic Camp) and deputy head of the Gulag. This work lauding slave labor is written in a tone of unabashed enthusiasm. As they vie to make the most striking comparisons, one of the authors has taken the trouble to calculate that from the rocks extracted during the construction of the White Sea Canal it would be possible to build seven pyramids of Cheops. The aptness of this comparison is confirmed by old photographs that show how the prisoners broke up huge blocks of stone by hand. One of them is holding a steel crowbar on the rock, while another hits it with a 10-kilogram hammer.

In Stalin's original plan, the White Sea Canal was to have above all strategic significance. The Generalissimo dreamed of moving naval warships from the Baltic to the Pacific via the White Sea and the Northern Seaway. But the White Sea Canal, built "in record time," was not suitable for this purpose. As he sailed on the steamship *Anokhin*, Stalin did not hide his

disappointment and curtly described the canal as "shallow and narrow," though he himself, just as curtly, had ordered it to be built "quickly and cheaply." Twenty months of murderous labor by tens of thousands of prisoners was all for nothing, and the despot was not happy with the canal. Two weeks after its official opening, Stalin gave orders for a new project to be designed, "the Great White Sea Canal," it was to be twice as deep, much wider than, and run parallel to the one already built. This time the preparations were thorough. The design work took three years, and was completed in 1936, but by then Stalin was already busy with other things – the Great Purge was on, and then the Second World War broke out. The big, fat volumes of calculations and designs for the Great White Sea Canal were left to gather dust in the archives.

[title page of the book]
Proletarians of all countries, unite!
The Stalin White Sea-Baltic Canal
A history of the Construction Project
edited by
M. Gorky, L. L. Auerbach, S. G. Firin
1934 "The History of Factories and Plants" State Publishing House

Peter the Great's "Monarch's Way" ended with a great victory – Russia had gained access to the Baltic Sea. The building of the White Sea Canal, however, ended in a total fiasco. The canal never played any strategic role. In 1941, when Finnish and Germans troops had occupied Medvezhegorsk and Povenets, Red Army sappers blew up the dams at the top of the watershed to withhold their advance. As a result, torrents of water flooded the enemy position, washing away the ancient wooden buildings of Povenets in the process. The economic importance of the White Sea Canal was and is marginal, especially because for six or seven months a year it is ice-bound.

For many years, citizens of the Soviet Union were reminded of Stalin's "great construction project" when they bought the popular *Belomory* ("White Sea") cigarettes each morning. The cigarette package has a map of the USSR, with three canals marked on it: the White Sea, the Moscow and the Volga-Don. All were built by Gulag prisoners. One can still buy *Belomory* cigarettes in just about any kiosk in Russia, and somehow no one is bothered by the fact that they bear the name of the canal whose construction cost thousands of human lives.

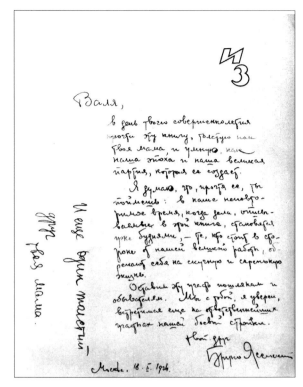

An inscription in *The Stalin White Sea-Baltic Canal* book by Bruno Jasieński, author of the chapter entitled "Finishing Off the Class Enemy."

Valia,
On the day of your coming of age, read this book, which is fat as your Mama and as wise as our era and our great party that created it.
    I think that, when you read it, you will understand: in our unforgettable era, when the things described in this book become everyday matters, those who stand aside from our great work will condemn themselves to a dull and nasty life.
    Let us leave that to the vulgarians and the bourgeois. We, I believe, shall meet again at the most responsible sentry posts of our own militant "construction project."

Your friend,
Bruno Jasieński
Moscow, February 18, 1934
and another fat friend,
your Mama

Bruno Jasieński, Polish writer and Futurist poet. He lived in the Soviet Union from 1929, was a member of the All-Union Communist Party (Bolshevik), and was shot in 1938. During the Great Purge the authorities withdrew the book from bookshops and libraries because OGPU Deputy Head Genrikh Yagoda, described in it as a man of great virtues, had been shot as a "right-wing Trotskyite" after a show trial in 1938.

Building one of the nineteen locks on the White Sea Canal.

Splitting rocks and drilling
holes for explosives.

Each prisoner had to extract
and remove from the canal
bed a daily quota of three
cubic meters of earth and
stone in order to fulfill the
norm; failing to fulfill it meant
a reduction in food rations.

The route of the White Sea
Canal was divided into nine
sections; construction was
carried out on all sections
simultaneously. Several
thousand prisoners worked
on each section.

Lighting bonfires to thaw the frozen ground.

Building a stone weir.

Heating mortar to help it bond in freezing weather.

Building a stone dam.

Working on the canal bed in winter.

Construction of Lock No. 3.

Building locks.

Wooden lock and dam structures. The basic material used to build the White Sea Canal was wood from the neighboring forests of Karelia.

Primitive pile-drivers driven by the muscle power of prisoners walking inside a wooden wheel.

"*Stakes are driven into the ground as follows. Large wheels are made, lined in planks, then four men walk inside them, and when the hammer-head rises to the desired height, a fifth man pulls on a line and the hammer-head falls, striking the stake. The maximum number of strikes that can be made in an hour is 10, or 100 strikes in a 10-hour working day. In the course of a day 1.5 stakes are driven in like this. Some 5,000 stakes have to be driven in.*"

Yakov Belenky to Genrikh Yagoda, March 1932.

OGPU's Special Construction Office laboratory in Medvezhegorsk.

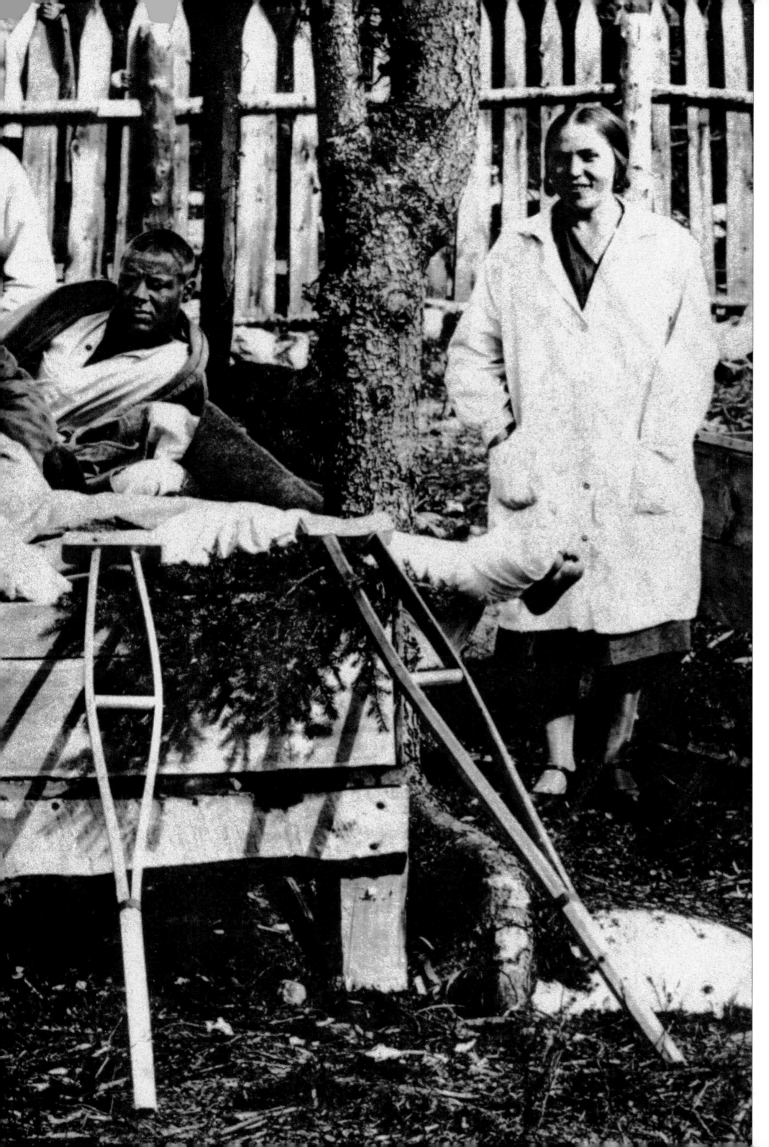

The camp hospital.
Prisoners fell ill and died
from exhaustion, malnutrition,
hypothermia in winter, terrible
sanitary conditions, and
work-related accidents.

Prisoners during a meal break.

A performance by prisoners from
the so-called *agit-brigade* or the
propaganda group. The slogans
read: "Let's deliver *Belomorstroi*
before the deadline", "Let's finish
the canal by October 1," and "Every
single one of us is a shock-worker".

The brass band playing for prisoners at work.

The sports club for the wives of heads of the
Construction of the White Sea-Baltic Waterway
Administration in Medvezhegorsk. In the middle row,
center, stands Jelisaveta Vasilewna, the wife
of Arseny Kuznetsov, Director of the *Belomorstroi*
Communications Division. The gymnastics were led
by prisoner Pavel Galubinsky (on the right), who
was shot in 1937 during the Great Purge. In fear
of repression, the Kuznetsovs scratched out his
face in their family album.

Officials of the White Sea Canal Construction Administration
in Medvezhegorsk, from left to right: Uspensky, Katelov,
Polozov, Kuznetsov, Dalinin.

Political training for employees of the White Sea Canal Construction Administration at Medvezhegorsk.
First on the left is Arseny Kuznetsov, Director of the *Belomorstroi* Communications Division.

Arseny Kuznetsov and
his friend, OGPU official
Sergei Dalinin.

Head of the Gulag Matvei Berman
(center, smiling) during an inspection
of the White Sea Canal in July 1932.

From right to left: construction manager of the White Sea Canal
Naftaly Frenkel, Head of the Southern Administration of *Belomorstroi*
Grigory Afanasiev, Head of the Gulag Matvei Berman. Second row,
third from the left in white shirt is K. Verzhbitsky, Deputy Chief
Engineer. Povenets, July 1932.

The villa where official guests of the
White Sea Canal stayed.

Alexei Tolstoi (in hat and glasses), one of the contributors to *The Stalin White Sea-Baltic Canal*, during a visit by Soviet writers to the construction site. Third from the left is Head of the Povenets construction area Piotr Borisov.

Soviet writer Demian Bedny
(center, smiling), one of the
contributors to *The Stalin
White Sea-Baltic Canal*,
during a visit to Lock No. 3.
To Bedny's right is Piotr
Borisov.

Prisoner Krasilnikov working on a portrait of Stalin
at the *Belomorstroi* Department of Culture and
Education, which was responsible for propaganda.

The *Karl Marx* during the opening ceremony for the Joseph Stalin White Sea-Baltic Canal, May 1933.

Dam at Sosnovets.

The White Sea Canal after opening for shipping.

Celebration held when basic construction was completed and the canal was filled with water, March 23, 1933.

One of the weirs regulating the water level.

THE WHITE SEA CANAL
Historical note

The White Sea Canal was built in 20 months between 1931 and 1933, connecting the city of Belomorsk and Lake Onega, as well as the Baltic and White Seas. The canal shortened the route from the Baltic to the White Sea, which formerly ran around the Scandinavian Peninsula, by 4,000 kilometers. However, in practice it did not fulfill its role because it was too shallow for sea-going vessels.

The canal is 227 kilometers long; 39 kilometers were cut out of the rock face, and the remaining 188 kilometers consist of dammed-up lakes and flooded riverbeds. There are 19 locks, 49 weirs and 15 dams. In all, there are over 100 hydraulic engineering structures.

The construction of the White Sea Canal opened a new chapter in the history of the Soviet Union. It was one of the first large economic projects to be done by inmates. Starting in the 1930s, prisoners held in the growing Gulag were used on a large scale to carry out economic tasks. The OGPU/NKVD changed its status from supplier of unpaid laborers to direct executor of works, and began to play an essential role in the USSR economy.

The number of inmates working at various times ranged from 60,000 to 100,000. About half were political prisoners, and the second largest group were peasants – victims of the collectivization of agriculture, and there were also common criminals. The precise number of victims is not known. According to cautious estimates, approximately 15,000 were killed.

1930

February 18: the USSR Labor and Defence Council passes a resolution to build the White Sea-Baltic Canal. Orders to implement the project are given to the People's Committee for Transport.
May 26: the Northern Region Construction Administration, Belomorstroi, is established, based in Medvezhegorsk.
The OGPU's Special Construction Office is created at the Lubianka in Moscow for prisoners who were qualified engineers and hydrologists. The design phase starts.
Summer: surveying the terrain and preparatory work are performed on site, involving 300 engineers, geologists and topographers, and 600 prisoners from the Solovetsky Special Purpose Camp.

1931

The annual average number of prisoners is 64,100.
Start of the year: the OGPU's Special Construction Office completes the design work.
At a session of the USSR Labor and Defence Council, Stalin states that the White Sea Canal must be built quickly and cheaply. All reinforced concrete and steel structures within the designs are replaced with wooden and stone ones to reduce costs. (Engineer O. V. Viazemsky designed the wooden Matkozhenskaia Dam, 150 meters long and 16 meters high; Engineer K.M. Zubrik designed the Shevanskaia Dam, and Professor V. N. Maslov the wooden lock gates, which worked for almost 50 years and were only replaced with steel ones in the 1970s. After construction was completed the three engineers were given an early release from the camps and awarded the Order of the Red Banner of Labor.)
The Northern Region Construction Administration, Belomorstroi, is transferred from the People's Committee for Transport to the OGPU and transformed into the Belomorstroi Construction of the White Sea-Baltic Waterway Administration under the management of Gulag head Lazar Kogan.
Genrikh Yagoda, Deputy Chairman of the OGPU, personally oversees the construction of the White Sea Canal.
Inmates are transferred from various camps to the construction area.
November 16: the White Sea-Baltic Corrective Labor Camp, Belbaltlag, is established, based in Medvezhegorsk. E. I. Sienkiewicz is appointed head of Belbaltlag.
N. Khrustalev is appointed Chief Construction Engineer, with Sergei Zhuk and K. Verzhbitsky as his deputies.
Construction begins.

1932

The annual average number of prisoners is 99,100.
P. F. Alexandrov is appointed head of Belbaltlag.
Intensive work continues along the entire length of the White Sea Canal.
June: The new Gulag head, Commissar for State Security Rank III Matvei Berman, takes on management of Belomorstroi.
Summer: OGPU Deputy Chairman Genrikh Yagoda visits the White Sea Canal and expresses satisfaction with the progress of the work.

1933

The annual average number of prisoners is 84,500.

Semion Firin is appointed head of Belbaltlag.

March 23: basic construction is completed and the canal is filled with water.

May 1: an opening ceremony is held for the White Sea Canal. Joseph Stalin cruises along the White Sea Canal, accompanied by Sergei Kirov and Kliment Voroshilov, on board the steamship *Anokhin*.

August 2: the USSR Council of People's Commissars passes a resolution declaring the White Sea Canal officially open for use.

August 17: in place of Belomorstroi a new prison camp/industrial complex is established, the OGPU White Sea-Baltic Combine, to service the canal, build ships and hydropower stations, clear forests and identify and utilize natural resources in the Karelian Republic, relying on the labor of prisoners from Belbaltlag and exiles.

The OGPU White Sea-Baltic Combine is ordered to design projects for two new canals: "The Great White Sea Canal" and the gigantic Kandalaksha-Murmansk canal bisecting the Kola Peninsula. (The designs were completed in 1935 and 1936, but they were never implemented.)

1941

The annual average number of prisoners is 71,270.

OGPU's White Sea-Baltic Combine is closed down.

1970s

The White Sea Canal is deepened from four to six meters, which allows larger river-sea ships with a cargo capacity of up to 3,000 tons to sail on it. Most of the wooden locks are replaced with reinforced concrete structures, and the wooden lock gates are replaced with steel ones.

Sources:

1. Ivan Chukhin, *Kanalarmeitsy, Istoria stroitelstva Belomorkanala* ["The Canal Army, a history of the construction of the White Sea Canal"], published by Karelia, Petrozavodsk 1990.
2. Sergei Krivenko, "The White Sea-Baltic ITL Corrective Labor Camp" in "The Prison Camps. An Encyclopedic Guide", issued by the Memorial Center for Research, Information and Dissemination (NIPC) in Moscow, jointly edited by Nikita Okhotin and Arseny Roginsky.

From a report by OGPU special plenipotentiary attached to the White Sea-Baltic Combine Yakov Belenky to Genrikh Yagoda, March 1932: *Sosnovets branch, 3,500 people, three* lagpunkty *[individual camps]. At the* lagpunkty *the women's barracks are situated in the middle of the camp. I shall not describe what goes on there, but in my opinion the camp as such is losing face. It is essential to divide off the women's barracks, and if necessary to surround them with barbed wire.*

From a file of Belbaltlag prisoners in the archives of the Ministry of Internal Affairs of the Karelian ASSR: Evgeny Sofitsky, born in 1886 in the village of Riazhaenskoe, Tambov province. A believer, sentenced to 10 years in the camps by the OGPU Board of the Central-Chernozemny [Black Earth] Region on February 26, 1930, under article 58.10 of the USSR Penal Code (counter-revolutionary propaganda and agitation). Died on May 5, 1933, in camp No. 21 of the OGPU's Belbaltlag department. Cause of death and place of burial unknown.

WHITE SEA CANAL
m e m o r i e s

Lock No. 6 today.

Lock gates and engine room.

Vitaly Alexandrov, Director of the White
Sea Canal Administration in his office in
Medvezhegorsk on Lake Onega.

A boat passing through
the lock.

Lock No. 1 at Povenets, with
Lake Onega beyond.

Galina Dovbania, keeper of Lock No. 2. In
the 1930s, during the collectivization of
agriculture, her parents were deported from
a village in Ukraine to the Karelian-Finnish
Republic and forced to work on construction
of the White Sea Canal. Galina Dovbania was
born in 1945 in Povenets, and has worked
on the canal since the early 1970s; a single
mother with three sons, she lives in the village
near the lock.

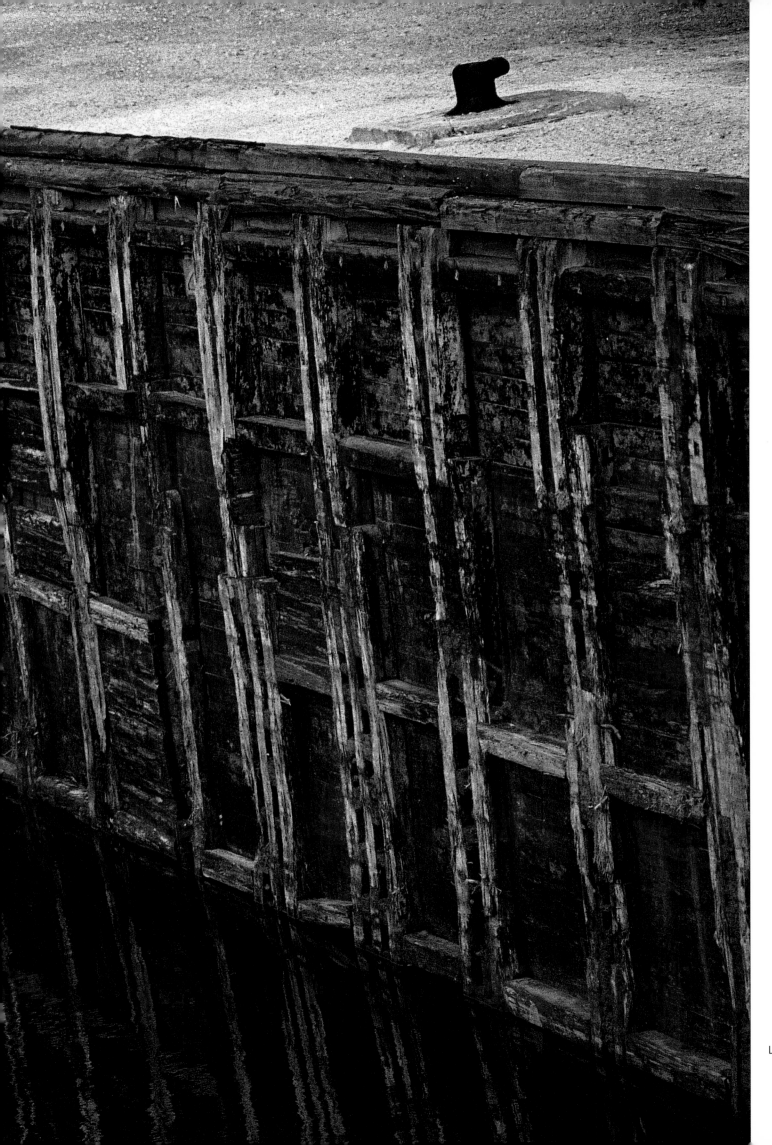

Lock No. 1 at Povenets.

Lock No. 8.

Nina Lilko, keeper of Lock No. 8.
In 1952 her parents came to the
White Sea Canal from Belarus in
search of better jobs. Nina Lilko
was born at the village near the
lock; she is a single mother with
two daughters.

The village near
Lock No. 9.

The dam at Sosnovets.

Piotr Sutormin, former
commander of the military
post that guarded Lock No. 9.
Now retired and single, he lives
in the village near the lock.

Underwater inspection and repair of lock gates.

Viktor Alexandrovich Kuznetsov,
director of Lock No. 9 since 1963;
his daughter and son-in-law work
as lock keepers.

Sailors on a ship sailing along the
White Sea Canal with a cargo of
fuel oil.

Olga Rogozhnikova, cook on a ship
sailing through the White Sea
Canal from Samara on the Volga
to Belomorsk.

Anastasia Kalinina, who used to
moor boats at Lock No. 9, retired.
When she was 15 her entire family
was deported from Ukraine to work
on construction of the White Sea
Canal. Since 1944 she has lived at
the village near Lock No. 9, and to
supplement her paltry pension she
picks mushrooms and berries that
she sells to sailors on ships
passing through.

Sergei Skripets, formerly employed
at Lock No. 9, was fired for
drunkenness, and now poaches
fur-bearing animals and elk. His
parents came to work on the White
Sea Canal to escape the famine in
the postwar years. Sergei Skripets
was born in 1958 at the village
near Lock No. 9; he is divorced
and has a teenage daughter who
lives near St. Petersburg.

The village near Lock No. 9.

A view of the town of Belomorsk on the White Sea, from the final nineteenth lock on the White Sea Canal.

Novaia
Zemlia

Kara Gates Strait

KARA
SEA

Vaigach Island

Varnek

Amderma

BARENTS
SEA

Yugorsky
Peninsula

Kara River

50 km

THE VAIGACH EXPEDITION

THE VAIGACH EXPEDITION
1930-1936

In July 1930, two steamships, the *Metel* and the *Gleb Boky*, set sail from Arkhangelsk and headed north. With the help of two ice-breakers, the *Malygin* and the *Sedov*, they crossed the White Sea and the Barents Sea. At daybreak on July 17 they sailed into Varnek Bay on the shore of the Arctic island of Vaigach. More than 100 prisoners disembarked from the ship, as well as a small detachment of soldiers, some professionals and the expedition leader, a well-regarded and highly decorated Chekist, Fiodor Eikhmans.

The prisoners began unloading cargo. Army tents were put up on shore, and portable iron stoves were fired up. The prisoners worked two 12-hour shifts, bringing ashore food supplies, coal, barrels of fuel and ready-made wooden houses. These homes were constructed in advance in Arkhangelsk, then dismantled and loaded onto the ships. From a height above the bay, these activities were witnessed by the astonished family of hunter Nikon Vylko, a member of the Siberian Nenets people, who lived in this place as nomads in tents made of reindeer hides.

By the end of the year the Varnek settlement was established on the island. On the low hills overlooking the bay, which are covered in green grass only during the short Arctic summer, stood a dozen or so wooden houses. These included the expedition's main headquarters, the army barracks, a bakery, a kitchen, a bathhouse, two prison barracks and an isolation cell. A smithy and a chemical laboratory were set up. The prisoners built a house on the hill, with a view of the settlement and the bay, for Fiodor Eikhmans and his deputy, Eduard Skaia.

The first mission of the OGPU's Vaigach Expedition was to prospect for and extract zinc and lead ore on the island. They were probably also counting on finding gold deposits there. The rumors about gold on Vaigach originated in an ancient northern Russian legend about "the golden woman," a Nenets idol made of gold. Legend had it that this statue was carried to the farthest northern reaches.

The Vaigach Expedition was in many respects a special event during the Gulag era. Apart from the fact that its participants were taken to the island against their will, it was more like a pioneer mining town in Alaska, or a trappers' trading post in Canada than a Soviet prison camp. There were no barbed wire fences or watchtowers, and outside work hours the prisoners were allowed to walk around the island freely. When they were sent into the tundra, they were given hunting rifles to protect themselves against polar bears while hunting for wildfowl. They were allowed to associate with the free workers without any restrictions and obtained their supplies at the same local shops, where they could buy sausages, cheese, chocolate and clothing.

The prisoners were properly fed and, in accordance with the dietary requirements for living in the Arctic, their diet was rich in vegetables to prevent scurvy. They also consumed large quantities of bread and herring, which they picked up at the local canteen. They had an eight-hour work day. Heated barracks, separate beds, clean bedding and winter clothes were all a source of astonishment for the prisoners who had come from other camps. For each daily work norm fulfilled, two days were written off a prisoner's sentence. Shock-workers, or workers who exceeded the norm, were paid cash prizes and allowed to bring their families to Vaigach.

After a few months a club was built where the prisoners' own musical and theatrical groups put on performances. Films were shown. In addition school was set up for the illiterate; geology courses were held; and the engineers gave popular science lectures. After work the prisoners could play chess at the club or visit the well-stocked library. In the winter skiing competitions were held.

The Vaigach Expedition had its own printing press. Supervised by Chekists, the prisoners published a propaganda newspaper whose Russian title *Udarnik* meant "The Shock-Worker," and a science-and-technology periodical, "Taming the Arctic," and two popular literary newspapers, "Aurora Borealis" and "The Gleam of Lead." There was also a wall newspaper called "The Arctic Depths."

In their spare time expedition heads Eikhmans and Skaia, who were passionate about hunting, used dog sleds driven by Nenets guides to hunt polar bears, Arctic foxes and wildfowl. Occasionally they hunted seals and white dolphins at sea.

The zinc and lead mines were built on Cape Razdelny on the far side of Varnek Bay, opposite the settlement. In the summer the prisoners traveled to work by boat, and in the winter they walked across the frozen bay. At first working conditions were very primitive. The prisoners were lowered in wooden buckets operated by manual winches into the pit, where they extracted ore-bearing rock with pickaxes. The ore was then transported to shore in wheelbarrows. During the navigation season, when the ice in Yugorsky Shar Strait melted, ships arrived at Varnek Bay, and new convoys of prisoners would disembark. After two years there were over a thousand prisoners on the island. The ore they mined was taken by boat to ships anchored in the harbor, which then took it back to Arkhangelsk.

Within the first few days after arriving in Vaigach Fiodor Eikhmans employed the Nenets to help with the expedition work. The Vylko, Taibare and Sobolev clans all took part. The indigenous peoples provided transportation in the form of sleds pulled by dogs and reindeer, and served as guides. They often visited the Varnek settlement, exchanged furs for everyday essentials and received medical attention. The expedition leader had a herd of 900 reindeer brought to the island and founded a reindeer breeding kolkhoz. The Chekists also established the Council of Vaigach Island, which they supervised with Nikon Vylko acting as chairman.

The exceptional nature of the Vaigach Expedition – the good treatment of the prisoners and their right to bring their families – was part of a government policy current at that time that aimed to colonize the far north and exploit its natural resources. But the atmosphere of the expedition must also have reflected the character of its leader who apparently was more of an adventurer than an executioner.

About a year after arriving in Vaigach, Fiodor Eikhmans met Galina Nikolaeva, the daughter of a former Czarist officer sentenced to 10 years in the camps. Before the revolution, her father, Emelian Nikolaev, had taken part in several Arctic expeditions and was therefore assigned the post of First Officer on the steamship *Malygin* after his arrest. The ship provided supplies for the Vaigach Expedition. In the summer of 1931 they were married in Arkhangelsk. For an OGPU officer to marry the daughter of a prisoner must have required great courage and determination. The newlyweds lived in the house on the hill with the view of Varnek Bay and spent several months together in Vaigach. By early 1932 all hope of finding gold had faded. After two years of intensive prospecting, only scanty deposits of zinc and copper were found. In April Eikhmans decided to return to Moscow, with good reason as his wife Galina was now pregnant. The famous Soviet Arctic pilot Fiodor Farikh came to fetch the couple, but during the flight to Arkhangelsk the airplane's engine broke down and it was forced to crash land in the tundra. The pilot and his passengers survived, and were helped by the local Nenets nomads. That August in Moscow Galina Eikhmans gave birth to a daughter, Elvira.

In the following years Fiodor Eikhmans worked for Soviet intelligence abroad, mainly in Japan. During the Great Purge in 1938, he was summoned to Moscow, arrested and shot. Galina, as an "enemy of the people," would not have escaped repression, were it not for the fact that she had earlier divorced Eikhmans. As a result an album of photographs from Vaigach survived, and is still preserved to this day by the daughter of the Vaigach Expedition leader, Elvira Eikhmans.

For over 50 years after the end of the Vaigach Expedition in 1936, the Varnek settlement was the base for a reindeer breeding sovkhoz (state farm) and a hunting kolkhoz (collective farm). After the Russian economy was reformed in the early 1990s, both institutions went bankrupt. Today about a hundred Nenets live on the island. They subsist on hunting, fishing and raising. Some receive paltry state pensions and child. Almost all the adults suffer from alcohol-related illnesses. There is no school, doctor or local authority representative at the settlement. A few houses have survived from the time of the Vaigach Expedition. The former expedition headquarters now houses a post office, telegraph station and private apartments. The former stables now house a food store, and the electric installation still has a generator that provides the settlement with electricity. It is operated by a Nenets, Sergei Valei, whose family lives in the house on the hill with a view of Varnek Bay—Fiodor Eikhmans' old quarters.

The Vaigach Expedition's hired workers, prisoners and Nenets.

An ice-breaker clearing the
way for a ship on the
Barents Sea, heading for
Vaigach Island.

Vaigach Island.

Vaigach Island.

A Nenets with a reindeer-drawn sled.

The inhabitants of Vaigach, the Nenets, are from a nomadic race of Siberian hunters and reindeer herders.

The Nenets on Vaigach Island.

Nenets Yakov Taibarei.

The Nenets believed in animism and shamanism. They called Vaigach *Hebidia Ya* – "The Holy Land." According to their beliefs, the island was home to the two chief gods of the Nenets pantheon, Vesako (the Old Man) and Hedako (the Old Woman). For centuries they held sacrificial ceremonies here, to which the Nenets made pilgrimages from distant regions of Western Siberia. Reindeer were sacrificed to their gods. During these rituals the Nenets set up wooden idols on the island. Only a few of these have survived, as most were burned by Orthodox missionary Vienyamin Smirnov in 1827.

Refuelling the airboat Komsiewierput at Varnek Bay.

Topographical work.

Building the Varnek settlement.

The forge.

The chemical laboratory.

Geologists.

Expedition guards.

Transporting ore from the
mine to the seashore in Cape
Razdelny. Preparing to load
ore-bearing rock onto ships.

Zinc and lead ore mine on Cape Razdelny.

Prisoners crossing the frozen Varnek Bay on their way to the mine. A rope stretched along posts helped find the way during blizzards. The settlement of Varnek can be seen on the horizon.

Funeral of prisoner Altanov. Varnek 1932.

Fiodor Eikhmans (right), Head of OGPU's Vaigach Expedition,
a Latvian, was born in 1897. He took part in the October
Revolution and worked for the Cheka from 1918 on. He was
director of the Solovetsy prison camp in 1924-1928, Gulag
head from April to June 1930, and was condemned to death
and shot in 1938. Eduard Skaia (left), Deputy Head, a Latvian.
He was Lenin's personal body guard in 1917-1918. During
the October Revolution, he was head of security at the
Bolshevik general staff, and later at the Bolshevik government
headquarters and at Lenin's apartment in the Smolny Institute
in Petrograd. He worked for the Cheka from 1918, and died
in Ukhtpechlag camp in 1938.

The editorial staff of the wall newspaper, "The Arctic Depths," produced by prisoners under Cheka supervision.

A variety show performed by prisoners at the Expedition club at Varnek settlement.

Chekists after hunting a white dolphin.

Eduard Skaia (lying on the sled)
and Nenets Gavril Taibarei.

Skinning a polar bear.

Fiodor Eikhmans (left) and
Eduard Skaia.

Galina, wife of Fiodor Eikhmans, at
home in Vaigach and out skiing with a
Chekist assigned to protect her from
polar bears.

Fiodor Eikhmans in a
polar bear fur.

The airplane taking Fiodor Eikhmans and his wife back to Arkhangelsk from Vaigach in April 1932 crashed. The group picture shows the survivors with the Nenets family who helped them. Galina Eikhmans is in the center, smiling. Pilot Fiodor Farikh is shown with the downed plane.

Trying to communicate via
the radio set removed from
the airplane.

THE VAIGACH EXPEDITION
Historical note

The OGPU's Vaigach Expedition was organized in 1930 to prospect for and mine polymetallic ores on the Arctic island of Vaigach, situated between the Barents and Kara Seas. The island is located between the Novaia Zemlia archipelago and the mainland, and forms two straits, the Kara Gates and the Yugorsky Shar, through which the Northern Seaway runs from Europe along the coast of Siberia and into the Pacific. For the Nenets – the aboriginal inhabitants of this region –Vaigach was the holy island of *Hebidiya Ya* and a site of sacrificial ceremonies.

Prisoners on the Vaigach Expedition did the following work:
- prospected on Vaigach Island, the Yugorsky Peninsula and the Kara Sea coast
- built and worked in zinc and lead mines and in an ore enrichment plant on Cape Razdelny
- built a copper mine on Dyrovaty Peninsula
- built a fluorite mine at Amderma
- built settlements at Varnek, Amderma and (partly) Khabarovo
- did topographical surveying and meteorological observation.

The Vaigach Expedition did not bring the expected results. The deposits of natural resources that were found were small and had no great economic significance. The Expedition did contribute to the assimilation of this region of the Arctic. In its peak period, the number of prisoners reached 1,500. The number of deaths has not been established. Considering the good diet, clothing and accommodation provided for the prisoners, the mortality rate was probably low.

Chronology

1921
The existence of zinc and lead ores on Vaigach Island is mentioned for the first time.

1925
Zinc and lead ores are discovered on Vaigach by geologist A. K. Shenkman during an expedition run by the USSR Academy of Sciences.

1927-1929
A. K. Shenkman leads a geological expedition, organized by the Arkhangelsk-based Commission for Cooperation with Minor Nations. He confirms that the zinc and lead deposits on Vaigach have industrial significance.

The island's inhabitants, about 100 Nenets, are registered at a kolkhoz for hunting and raising reindeer.

1930
April: the Politburo of the Central Committee of the All-Union Communist Party (Bolshevik) discusses the question of mining the polymetallic ore deposits on Vaigach Island.

May: the Vaigach Expedition is organized by OGPU's central staff by order of the USSR government, with financial and economic management under the direct control of the OGPU in Moscow.

Fiodor Eikhmans is appointed head of the Expedition. The OGPU's Administration of Special Purpose Northern Camps assembles a contingent of prisoners, recruits hired workers and organizes Expedition security guards. Specialists including geologists, mining engineers and topographers, are transferred to Arkhangelsk from various camps.

July 17 — the first group of Expedition members — 125 prisoners, between 10 and 20 guards, and 7 freely hired specialists — disembarks on Vaigach Island in Varnek Bay.

Geological prospecting is conducted on the island. Two small zinc and lead deposits are discovered. Preparations are made to mine deposits discovered earlier at Cape Razdelny on Varnek Bay.

Varnek settlement, the Expedition base, is built. The accommodation buildings are completed before the onset of winter.

1931
In September the number of prisoners is 334.

The mine is constructed and the extraction of zinc and lead ore begins at Cape Razdelny. The Nenets Sobolev discovers copper ore deposits with traces of gold, silver and platinum on Dyrovaty Peninsula at the northern end of the island. A mine is built in this spot.

Autumn: Fiodor Eikhmans brings his wife Galina to the island.

1932
In December the number of prisoners is 1,100.

New Expedition head Alexander Ditskaln, a Latvian, arrives on Vaigach. Six new prison barracks, a powerhouse and a club are built.

April: Fiodor Eikhmans and his wife leave the island.

Working conditions in the mine at Cape Razdelny undergo major improvement with the installation of electric lighting in the tunnels, electric lifts and pneumatic hammers. A zinc-lead ore enrichment plant starts to operate alongside the mine.

Twelve brigades of prisoners led by geologists prospect for polymetallic ores on the island and the mainland (the Yugorsky Peninsula and the Kara Sea coast). A rich deposit of fluorite is discovered on the western coast of the Kara Sea near the mouth of River Amderma.

The Vaigach Expedition buys a 50-ton motorized sailing schooner named *Vaigach*. Prisoner Egon Bergolts is appointed captain (shot in 1938).

1933

There is no data on the number of prisoners.

A natural history museum opens at Varnek settlement, with a collection of geological and zoological specimens, a herbarium of local flora, photographs and maps.

Expedition inmates and equipment are transferred from Vaigach to Amderma, 70 kilometers away on the mainland, where they start to build a fluorite mine.

1934

In January the number of prisoners is 1,498.

Sergei Sidorov is appointed head of the OGPU's Vaigach Expedition (later known as the Vaigach Separate Camp Site).

The Vaigach Expedition is charged to build the northern section of the Vorkuta-Yugorsky Shar Strait railroad (220 kilometers). Prisoners start to build a pier for ships and the settlement of Khabarovo on the Yugorsky Peninsula as a base for construction of the railroad. (The railroad was not completed in the 1930s or later.)

August 10: the Vaigach Expedition is reorganized and separated into two units: the economic West Arctic Combine, under the auspices of the Northern Seaway Administration, and the prison camp – the Vaigach Separate Camp Site.

1935

On January 1, the number of prisoners is 1,211.

The mine on Cape Razdelny floods with water. All mining work and prospecting on the island is suspended. All the prisoners, mining equipment, building materials and food supplies are evacuated from Vaigach to the settlement at Amderma.

1936

On January 1, the number of prisoners is 1,092.

October 17: the Vaigach Separate Camp Site is closed down. The prisoners are transported to Arkhangelsk on the steamship *Krasnoe Znamya*. The abandoned Varnek settlement is occupied by the Vaigach kolkhoz for reindeer breeding and by about 100 Nenets.

1990s

The Soviet hunting and reindeer-breeding kolkhoz goes bankrupt.
The number of inhabitants on the island is about 100 Nenets.

Sources :

1. Irina Flige, *Osoblag Vaigach* ["Vaigach Separate Camp"], in *Vestnik Memoriala*, Moscow 1999.

2. Konstantin Gursky, *Moi Vaygach* ["My Vaigach"], published by *Nenetsky okruzhnoi kraevedchesky muze*i "the Nenets District Local History Museum"], Naryan-Mar 1999.

3. Sergey Krivenko, *Vaigatskaia Ekspeditsia OGPU* ["OGPU's Vaigach Expedition"] in *Lagry.* ["The Prison Camps. An Encyclopedic Guide"], issued by the "Memorial" Center for Research, Information and Dissemination (NIPC) in Moscow, jointly edited by Nikita Okhotin and Arseny Roginsky.

4. *Ostrov Vaigach. Kulturnoe i prirodnoe nasledie* ["Vaigach Island. Cultural and Natural Heritage"], vol. 1, edited by P. Boiarsky and V. Stoliarova, *Trudy Morskoi arkticheskoi kompleksnoi ekspeditsii* (MAKE) ["Transactions of the Arctic Sea Complex Expedition (MAKE)"], Moscow 2000.

5. Irina Reznikova, *Vaigach*, in historical quarterly *Karta* No. 18, Warsaw 1996.

At times it was hard. In the spring we were blinded by the constant, low and very bright light. We were given protective dark glasses, but there weren't enough of them. The contrast between the dark mine and the glittering snow had a bad effect on our sight. In the summer we were tormented by mosquitoes and in the winter by the frost. A lot of people were frostbitten. People were killed in the mine because elevator cables broke or tunnels caved in. Yet I always felt as if most of us were bewitched by the "romance" of it. I can't remember anyone around me ever losing heart.

Vatslav Dvorzhetsky, a prisoner on OGPU's Vaigach Expedition

This tragedy happened in Vaigach in the fall of 1932. In Varnek Bay, about 700 meters from shore opposite the settlement, an old steamship was anchored in the harbor for the third day in a row. Machinery, food, hay, fuel, barrels of grease and coal had already been unloaded onto shore. Zinc ore was being loaded on board and suddenly the temperature dropped sharply. We could see the layers of sea-ice rising on the surface of the bay, and the cutters running between landing place and the ship were moving more and more slowly. A cutter towing three boats full of prisoners was laboriously, meter by meter, breaking its way through a thick layer of ice to the shore. When it was about 100 meters from shore, the engine refused to work. The cutter and the boats were stuck, imprisoned in the ice. All attempts to break through to the shore proved fruitless. Hour after hour went by. Soon it grew dark. The people on the boats were shouting, begging for help. A searchlight was rigged up on the shore. A second cutter, which was anchored by the dock, could not move from the spot. Gangways were built on the shore, but the planks couldn't take the weight of a man and at once sank into the sea-ice. An extremely strong blizzard started to blow, with a low wind, which made the situation of the prisoners on the ice even worse. On the shore people kept watch the whole time, despairing at their inability to help the dying men. Only on the third day did the bay freeze up enough for the first daredevils to cross the planks and reach the site of the tragedy, where they found only the engineer and helmsman still alive. They survived because they were inside the cutter's enclosed pilothouse and had a blowlamp to keep themselves warm. The other 24 men on the boats froze to death.

Konstantin Gursky, a prisoner on OGPU's Vaigach Expedition

A big event in our lives was the First All-Nenets Congress of Councils. It is hard to imagine or describe the impression our "wonders" made on them. They were especially delighted by the brass band – it was the first time they had ever seen one. I shall never forget one old Nenets woman. The festive sound of the "Internationale," and then the march from Wagner's opera Tannhäuser, *sent her into a state of unimaginable ecstasy. Tears flowed from her wide-open eyes, and there was a look of rapture on her wrinkled, weather-beaten face.*

Konstantin Arkhangelsky, a prisoner on OGPU's Vaigach Expedition

Quotes from: historical quarterly *Karta* No. 18, Warsaw 1996.

Remains of the Vaigach Expedition on the shore of
Yugorsky Shar Strait, in the Barents Sea.

Remains of the Vaigach
Expedition at the former
settlement of Khabarovo
on Yugorsky Peninsula.

Vestiges of the zinc and
lead mine at Cape Razdelny.

The settlement at Varnek.
Inhabitants of the house where
the Vaigach Expedition had its
headquarters. In the 1930s the
building housed offices and a radio
station; now it includes private
apartments, a post office and
telegraph station.

Fiodor Eikhmans' house and its
present occupants – Nenets
Sergei Valei and his son Roman.

Nenets hunter Alexei Taibarei; his father
worked for the OGPU Vaigach Expedition.

Headman of Varnek settlement, Ivan Valei.

Nenets hunters, brothers Nikolai
and Andrei Vylko.

Nenets hunters, brothers
Pasha and Aliosha Taibarei.

Olga Valieysky
and her son,
from a family
of reindeer
breeders.

Hunter Pavel (Pasha) Taibarei.

The ancient Nenets idol was returned to Vaigach after restoration at the Russian Institute for Cultural and Natural Heritage in Moscow. The Varnek settlement headman, Alexei Valei, and brothers Nikolai and Andrei Vylko set it up in its old place on Bolshoi Tsynkovy Island on the western shore of Vaigach.

Varnek settlement.

Varnek settlement.

Sergei Valei and the generator
that supplies the settlement
with electricity.

Daily life in Varnek.

Hunting geese in spring.

Hand-painted cover of a
theatre program from Section
Five of the Kuznetsk
Correctional Labor Camp,
1957.

THE THEATER IN THE GULAG

Ticket price: one ruble. No entry into the auditorium after the third bell, said the theater program at Salekhard, a Siberian town in the Arctic Circle. It was 1948, and Nikolai Strelnikov's operetta *The Countrywoman* was being performed. In the first rows sat the camp bosses and prison guard officers, in uniforms and polished boots, with their wives in evening gowns. Behind them sat the commissaries, engineers, chauffeurs and cooks. After the performance, in the dressing room the actors took off their prince's, lady's and hussar's costumes and changed into padded jackets and earflap hats. In the gloom of the Arctic night, an armed convoy escorted the conductor, musicians, actors and dancers behind the barbed wire again. Here the performers went back to their real-life roles – as prisoners.

The patron of the theater was Colonel of State Security Vasily Barabanov, head of the Northern Camp Railroad Construction Administration. Under his command, tens of thousands of prisoners were building the line from Salekhard to Igarka, later known as the Road of Death. Barabanov's theater was fully professional. It was housed in a specially erected building, and the lighting, costumes and props were bought at the Bolshoi Theater in Moscow. The chief director, serving a 10-year sentence, was Leonid Obolensky, a film director who had worked with Sergei Eisenstein. The symphony orchestra consisted of over 30 musicians under the leadership of Nikolai Cherniatynsky, who before his arrest was the chief conductor at the Odessa opera. The orchestra performed with an operetta ensemble, a ballet company, a choir and soloists. Zinovy Binkin, a graduate of the Moscow Conservatory and during the war conductor of the Red Army Representative Orchestra, ran a variety show which included a jazz band, performers and a magician. There was also a small company of actors who put on plays.

Within the Gulag camps there were dozens of theaters, whose actors were prisoners, often leading performers. In the Komi Republic alone, besides Barabanov's ensemble, there were camp theaters at Vorkuta, Vologda, Ukhta, Inta and Kniazhpogost. Professional theaters operated in Magadan, Norilsk, Salekhard, Medvezhegorsk, and on the Solovetsky Islands. It was the ambition of many camp heads to have their own theater, especially those in the far north, for whom the theater was the only entertainment – besides vodka – in their isolated world. Grigory Litinsky, a Moscow writer who, as a prisoner, worked in the theater administration at Vorkuta, mentioned that the prison camp officials were in the habit of going to the theater every night as if to a restaurant. "They would listen to a favorite aria and then go back to the buffet to quench their thirst with champagne. The top brass had their own private room in the theater, where they were brought alcohol and snacks."

The theater at Vorkuta was called the USSR NKVD *Vorkutstroi*'s Theater of Music and Drama and was under the command of General Mikhail Maltsev. The director was Boris Mordvinov, former chief director of Moscow's Bolshoi Theater. Stars of the Soviet stage performed there, including the popular favorite of those years, Valentina Tokarskaia. In 1944 the head of *Vorkutstroi*, General Maltsev, wrote to a friend, "The theater is coming. Recently it's been restocked with valuable new people from the transit camps, and it's looking very promising."

Maltsev's theater put on dramas, comedies and operas, such as *The Queen of Spades*, *Boris Godunov*, *La Traviata* and *Faust*. But the most popular shows were the operettas, including Dunaevsky's *Free Wind*, Hervé's *Nitouche* and Kálmán's *The Violets of Montmartre*. They were shown over and over again, *The Gypsy Princess* over a hundred times.

Apart from the repertoire of entertainments and operettas, propaganda dominated the camp stages: *The Song of the Leader* was sung, *A Word to Comrade Stalin* was recited and the anniversaries of the October Revolution were celebrated. Shows were put on to "teach revolutionary vigilance and burning hatred towards our enemies." In one of them the heroine "finds the inner strength and courage to recognize that her beloved is an enemy," as the reviewer, Sviatukhin, wrote in *Sovetskaia Kolyma* about a show called *Premature Love* at the Magadan theater. The dramatic repertoire was dominated by plays glorifying the victory of the proletariat and denouncing "world imperialism," but also featured selected works by Russian writers, including Ostrovsky, Gogol, Griboedov and, of course, Gorky.

So-called concerts were organized in the camps for the prisoners. Prisoners would put on a variety show on a makeshift stage in the camp dining room. The performers sang, danced, and recited poetry by Mayakovsky, acrobats put on a display and a magician showed off his skills. The official claim was that the variety shows were supposed to raise the prisoner's labor productivity. In keeping with the spirit of the age, performance norms were set for camp theaters, which they had to fulfill and surpass. The newspaper *Sovetskaia Kolyma* dated September 2, 1937 wrote, "July 19. The performance logbook proudly displays the number 53. The plan has already been surpassed by six shows! August 23. Magadan. The results of our theater company's tour can now be summed up. Along the way we gave 99 performances. If we add to this the 80 shows and 65 concerts that our other theater company gave for the Southern Camp Administration, we get an impressive sum." At the same time vast numbers of prisoners were being executed in the camps at Kolyma as part of the Great Purge, which claimed almost 12,000 victims.

Performers for the theaters were collected at transit camps, where newly arrived prisoners were sorted before being sent to work. There, from the nameless mass of prisoners, pouring in from all over the country, the performers were picked out. The most promising consignments were from Moscow and Leningrad – that was where the real celebrities were found. The person who made the selection worked for the camp theater, and was most likely a prisoner too, given full authority to act on behalf of the NKVD patron. For artists, the theater was their salvation, because working on stage was not the same as felling forests up to their waist in snow, nor was it like mining, or unloading wagons in the cold, where those unaccustomed to physical work in tough conditions, sensitive people with little psychological resilience, were the first to perish. Alexei Morov, artistic director of Colonel Barabanov's theater, used to say to the actors, "Our salvation lies in the fact that we can devote ourselves entirely to work. We should forget that behind the stage there's a man with a machine gun. Our work, our art is everything. The role, the notes, the music."

Performers who did not have the good fortune to end up in the theater disappeared in the anonymous mass of prisoners grinding away at physical labor for 12 hours a day. Their fate varied. Painter Piotr Bendel began his career as chief set designer for the *Vorkutstroi* theater by drawing the portrait of a guard on a cigarette packet. Then he painted portraits of the camp bosses, until he was transferred to the theater at Vorkuta. The prominent Russian painter Vasily Shukhaev, who had exhibited in New York, Paris and London, did physical labor for two years in the camp at Kolyma. He was saved by his wife Vera, who managed to arrange his transfer to Magadan when he was already extremely emaciated. There he worked for eight years as a set designer at the USSR NKVD *Dalstroi*'s Gorky Theater of Music and Drama in Magadan.

Not everyone was as lucky. Sergei Amaglobeli, the manager of Moscow's Maly Theater, died in a camp. The actor Boris Alexandrov did not survive his eight-year sentence. Lesh Kurbas, the Ukrainian director, theater reformer and founder of the Berezil Theatre Company based in Kharkov, was shot at Solovki. After coming out of the camps, set designer Boris Erbstein and pianist Vsevolod Topilin, accompanist for the famous violinist David Oistrakh, both took their own lives. Vsevolod Meyerhold and the Georgian director Alexandr Akhmateli were both shot. Salomon Michoels, manager and artistic director of the Moscow Jewish/Yiddish Chamber Theatre died in an automobile accident in Moscow, presumably on orders from Stalin. Others who perished in the camps include Tatar playwright Fatki Burnash, director Veniamin Zuskin, film actor Kiril Ivanov, theater expert Adrian Petrovsky, opera singer Vladimir Zubkov-Shustruisky, director Karim Tinchurin, pianist and soloist of the Moscow Philharmonic Ada Milikovskaia, playwrights Viktor Savin, Sergei Tretiakov, Fiodor Chesnokov and many others.

Sources :

The author's interviews with actors from the camp theaters: Nina Gamilton, Tamara Petkievich, Valentina Tokarskaia, Platon Nabokov, Ivan Rusinov and Lazar Sheryshevsky.

Alexandr Kozlov, *Teatr na Severnoi Zemle* ["The Theater in the Northern Land"], Magadan 1992.

Viktor Kuzin, *Martirolog* ["A Martyrology"] in the bi-weekly periodical *Teatralnaia zhizn* ["Theatrical Life"] No 13, 1989.

Teatr Gulaga. Vospominania, ocherki. ["The Gulag Theater. Memories and sketches"], edited by Marlen Korallov, published by Memorial, Moscow 1995.

The prisoners' agit-brigade putting on a propaganda performance, known as the "live newspaper," for prisoners working on the construction of the White Sea Canal. Karelian Republic, 1932.

The entrance to the theater at the Solovetsky camp. The sign reads "Solovetsky Section I Theater" (Section I of the Solovetsky Special Purpose Camp). Solovetsky Monastery, 1927.

We attended a performance at the theater, which is apparently housed in the former monastery refectory. It seats 700 people, tightly packed in, of course. The performance was very interesting and varied. A very small but good "symphony orchestra" played the overture from The Barber of Seville*: a violinist played a mazurka by Wieniawski and* Spring Waters *by Rachmaninoff; the prologue from* I Pagliacci *was quite well sung. They then performed some Russian songs and dances, as well as a "cowboy" and an "eccentric" dance. Someone recited Zharov's* Harmony *superbly, accompanied by an accordion and a piano. The troupe of acrobats put on a stunning show – five men and one woman – and did tricks you wouldn't even see in a good circus. During intermissions a large brass band superbly played pieces by Rossini, Verdi and Beethoven in the foyer.*

Maxim Gorky, in his article entitled "Solovki"
written after visiting the camp in 1929.

Poster advertising a camp performance in 1927:
SLON Section I Theater
The Solovetsky Special Purpose Camp
on Saturday, June 9, and Sunday June 10
will present
The Calm
a play in 8 scenes by V. N. Bill-Belotserkovsky
performed by the entire company
produced by Chief Director B. Glubokovsky
Assistant Director Gazalius
BRASS BAND
led by Speransky
ticket prices from 15 kopeks to 1 ruble

Finale of the Second Prisoners'
Amateur Talent Show. Central
Asian Labor Camp
Administration, Uzbek Republic,
1950s.

Rehearsal for a performance of Maxim Gorky's play
The Lower Depths at the Solovetsky Special Purpose
Camp theater. Solovetsky Monastery, 1928.

A display by the prisoners' agit-brigade
at the White Sea Canal construction
site, Karelian Republic, 1931-1933.

Prison actors of the camp theater, prison complex
Donlag, Dowbas, 1949.

Zinovy Binkin's jazz band (he is the
trumpet player sitting above the letter A).
The letters in the foreground spell "jazz."
The theater of Colonel Arseny Barabanov,
head of the Northern Camp
Administration of Railroad Construction.
Salekhard, Tiumen oblast, northwestern
Siberia, circa 1948.

Zinovy Binkin at the piano, and third from the left Lazar Shershevsky, literary assistant at Colonel Arseny Barabanov's theater. Salekhard, Tiumen oblast, northwestern Siberia, circa 1948.

Lazar Sheryshevsky, poet, member of the Writers' Union, and prisoner in the Gulag camps from 1944-1949. After his release from the camps, he was not allowed to leave Salekhard, so he worked at the cultural center. After Stalin's death, in 1953 he finally returned to his mother in the city of Gorky, where he went to university. He lives in Moscow.

All summer and fall, right up to the beginning of the period of perpetual darkness, Zinovy Binkin's band performed along the route of the railroad under construction. Two "teplushki" were provided – freight cars with iron stoves and one watchman per car – and off we went. When we reached the end of the railroad track, we went to the more distant camps on foot. At that point we established an order for carrying heavy objects: the double-bass, percussion instruments and costume trunks. We played at settlements for free workers and in camp canteens and barracks for prisoners. Our audience would sit or lie on two-story wooden bunks, exhausted after the day's work. The actors performed skits and recited poetry, and Binkin's Jazz Band played. At first we used to play American jazz classics, until the censors banned them, but Russian jazz was quite well developed by then, so we played the national repertoire.

A superb magician used to perform with us – Nikolai Krotov; he was a great master of his art, and his best trick of all was that one day he quite simply vanished – he escaped on our way to a concert.

Nina Gamilton was a ballet dancer at the Bolshoi
Theater and a prisoner in the Kolyma camps
from 1937-1942. After her release from the
camps she was not allowed to leave Kolyma.
Until 1947 she performed at the USSR NKVD
Dalstroi's Gorky Theater of Music and Drama in
Magadan. She returned to Moscow 10 years
after her arrest. For many years she was
involved in education. She died in 1997.

Nina Gamilton after a performance of *Spring* in Moscow. USSR NKVD
Dalstroi's Gorky Theater of Music and Drama, Magadan, 1943.

Nina Gamilton on stage
at the camp theater at
Kolyma, 1940-1942.

In *September 1937 I was performing Swan Lake at the
Bolshoi Theater in Moscow. We had left a meeting at
the Actors' Club late at night. I got home and there
was a search going on; everything had been turned
upside down. There in my apartment sat a goon from
the NKVD and my mother, white as a sheet. They
arrested me, I got five years and ended up at Kolyma
in a camp full of criminals. They swore appallingly.
There was nothing but frozen potatoes to eat. I
thought I'd go mad. Luckily, I soon got into the camp
theater.*

*They were lacking professional performers. Apart from
me, there was one other female dancer, two vocalists
and an actor. We put on a ballet about the war in
Spain. I played the part of Dolores Ibarruri, and the
choir cried, "No pasaran." There was no orchestra,
but two pianists played the music, Maria Gordon and
Sofia Herbst, a first-rate pianist who studied at the
Moscow Conservatory. Later on she hanged herself in
the camp.*

*When they released me from the camp five years later
in 1942, they bought me a sealskin coat and
something else as well, so that I'd look good. For them
it was a matter of prestige. How could they let a
ballerina from the Bolshoi Theater leave their camp in a dirty padded jacket? Later on of
course, once I started to earn a living, I had to give them the money back. And the fur was
stolen from me anyway in the very first week of my freedom.*

*I worked in the theater in Magadan as a free person, but without the right to leave Kolyma.
They assigned prisoners to me as maids. They lived at home with me and didn't go back to
the camp at night. The camp bosses used the prisoners for everything – a pedicure,
manicure or haircut. They'd summon a tailor-prisoner to their home if they needed to have
some sewing done, and cooks, when a large party was being prepared. Prisoners with light
sentences served the bosses; for instance, "a family member of a traitor to the fatherland,"
that is, somebody imprisoned for the alleged crimes of a relative. My friend, an intelligent,
educated woman, worked for the head of Dalstroi, Ivan Nikishov, as a cook*

Nina Gamilton

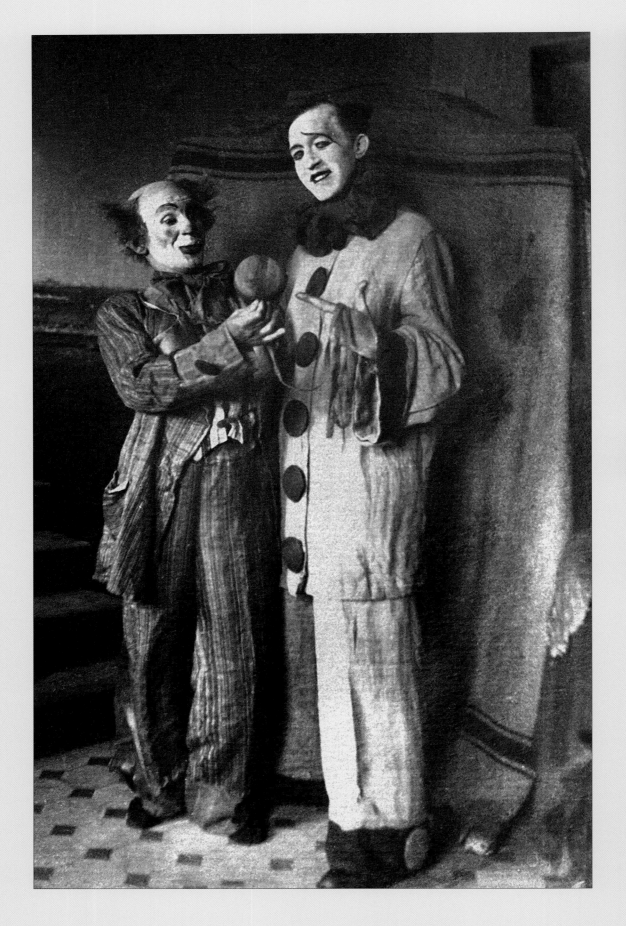

The camp puppet theater, run by prisoner Tamara Tsulukidze. Northern Railroad Corrective Labor Camp, Kniazhpogost, Komi Republic, date unknown

Prisoners Grigory Azarov and Yury Osabchy in a scene from "Clownery on local themes." The theater at the Leningrad Oblast Corrective Labor Camps Administration, 1946.

Tamara Tsulukidze was arrested in 1937 together with her husband, the director Alexandr Akhmateli, and sentenced to 10 years in the camps. Akhmateli was shot soon after his arrest. For several years she worked at forestry sites and stone quarries before ending up in Colonel Shemen's camp theater at Kniazhpogost in the Komi Republic, where she ran the puppet theater. She performed at settlements for free workers and in the camps for children born in prison as the result of rape, camp love affairs or the mercenary activities of criminal female prisoners who became pregnant in order to get into the camp for nursing mothers. In 1955, after 18 years of camps and exile, Tamara Tsulukidze returned to the theater of her youth, the Rustaveli Theater in Moscow. The first job she got was the role of Lenin's mother in the propaganda play *The Family*. She died in 1990.

The children were extremely thin, gloomy and fearful, with their little heads shaved bare. They stared in silence. In a narrow corridor in the accommodation block, which served as a "playroom," about 50 children were sat on the floor in front of the puppet theater curtain. The show began. When Petrushka the cat appeared they didn't react at all. Total silence. But when Druzhok the dog appeared above the curtain and barked, they were terrified. The front rows began to howl, and the rest followed them. I came out in front of the curtain to show them it was only a puppet, but it was no use – they just went on crying. Children brought up in the "zone" had never seen a cat, a cockerel or a cow, and they associated a dog with the guards' dogs.
Once, after a performance of Andersen's story The Nightingale, a four-year-old boy came up to me, pulled me by the skirt and said, "Auntie, I love you."

Tamara Tsulukidze

Camp theater dressing room.
Solovetsky Islands, 1927.

This and the following pages feature hand-colored photographs of the variety show of Kuznetsk Corrective Labor Camp Section V, 1957.

A "Russian dance" performed by the camp theater group. Hand-colored photograph. Krasnogorsk, 1957.

Satirical Songs on Everyday Themes.
V. Barsuk (left) and P. Sharov accompanying him on the accordion.

A scene from the skit *Life's Little Trifles*.
Performers: Y. Zhukov and Y. Troshikov.

A performance of *Gravity*.
From left to right: V. Varenik, Y. Troshikov, V. Shilenko, A. Bulatov, N. Vologdin.

A performance of *Gravity*. From left to right: V. Shilenko, P. Sharov, A. Bulatov, Y. Troshikov, V. Varenik, N. Vologdin, A. Dubinin.

A performance of *Gravity*.
A. Dubinin (left) and A. Bulatov (right).

The variety show performers of
Kuznetsk Corrective Labor Camp Section V.

A. F. Dubinin, director of the company.

Valentina Tokarskaia (center) on stage at the USSR NKVD Vorkutstroi's Theater of Music and Drama in the musical *The Violets of Montmartre* by Imre Kálmán. Vorkuta, mid-1940s.

Valentina Tokarskaia in Odessa, 1925.
Valentina Tokarskaia and Andrei
Gaidarov in a scene from *The Tango of
Death*. Tashkent, 1920. Valentina
Tokarskaia met Gaidarov 25 years later
in Vorkuta, where he worked as a
prisoner in the camp theater.

Valentina Tokarskaia
in Kiev, 1928.

Valentina Tokarskaia was a movie actress and star of the Moscow music hall in the 1930s. She was born the daughter of an operetta singer in Kharkov. Her father was a Pole, and her mother a Russian German. From the age of 14 she performed on the stage and with traveling troupes. She became popular when she played the lead role in one of the first Soviet film comedies, *The Marionettes*. During the war she performed for Red Army soldiers. When her company was captured by the Germans, she also performed for them. After returning to the Soviet Union in 1945, Valentina Tokarskaia was sentenced to five years in the camps for "collaboration with the enemy." She served her sentence in Vorkuta, and performed at the USSR NKVD Vorkutstroi's Theater of Music and Drama. There she began a relationship with Alexei Kapler, a famous journalist and screenwriter who was also serving a sentence in Vorkuta. Kapler ended up in the camp because he had flirted with Stalin's daughter, Svetlana Alliluieva. Because he objected to this, Stalin had Kapler sent to the camps. After her release from the camp in 1949, Valentina Tokarskaia was not allowed to live in Moscow. She continued to work at the Vorkuta theater as a free performer. She and Alexei Kapler returned to the capital together only after Stalin's death in 1953. Tokarskaia was hired by the Theater of Satire in Moscow, where she performed until well into old age. She died in 1995.

The music hall shows in Moscow were wonderful, with magnificent, fairytale costumes. When we used to put on variety shows there, 30 dancing girls performed on stage. Every day we had a completely full house. Despite our success, one day the authorities said the music hall was of no interest to our nation and changed it to the People's Theater [of Creative Arts], which no one ever went to, of course.
When I performed in the music hall, the ladies used to keep their husbands far away from me, because for some unearthly reason they were convinced that I could seduce any man I laid eyes on. And when Alexei and I came back to Moscow from Vorkuta, those ladies used to whisper to one another, "Just think – even in the camps she managed to bill and coo, and who did she get? Kapler!"
After our return to Moscow, Svetlana Alliluieva called me and suggested we meet. We arranged to meet in the foyer of the Theater of Satire on Mayakovsky Square. Alliluieva asked me if I would give Kapler back to her. I was astounded. I replied, "That's a matter between the two of you. If that's what he wants, he'll leave me himself." And he did. But many years later, and for a different woman.

Valentina Tokarskaia

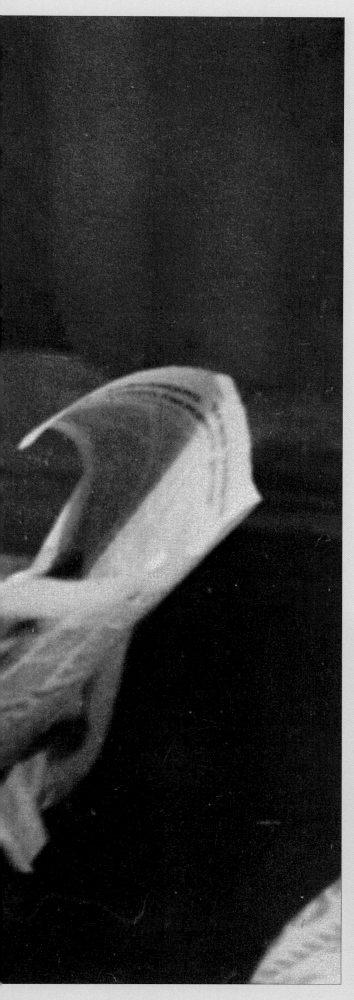

Valentina Tokarskaia in a photo taken by Alexei Kapler, who worked at the Vorkuta theater as a photographer. In his photography studio Kapler installed a secret room behind the doors of a wall cupboard, where he could receive Tokarskaia.

Valentina Tokarskaia in the role of an Indian in the musical *Rose-Marie*, Vorkuta, 1946-1949.

Valentina Tokarskaia and Alexei Kapler in Moscow, 1960s.

Valentina Tokarskaia at the age of 85
on stage at the Moscow Theater of Satire
in *Be Quiet, Sadness, Be Quiet*.

Ivan Rusinov, an actor from Moscow's Yermolov Theater. In the 1930s, as a prisoner he performed on stage for the theater at the White Sea Canal Construction Administration in Medvezhegorsk and at the Solovetsky camp theater.

A special feature of the White Sea Canal Central Theater was that the bosses wanted to see the widest possible variety of shows, in order to have the greatest pleasure. Because of this the repertoire was as follows: on Monday – a drama, on Tuesday – an opera, on Wednesday – an operetta, on Thursday – a ballet, on Friday – a symphony concert (the orchestra had about 50 musicians), on Saturday - variety shows and skits, and on Sunday – a new film.

Every time I performed on stage, the daughter of Sergei Zhuk, Deputy Chief Engineer for the White Sea Canal, used to turn up in the auditorium. Before the show I would peep out from behind the wings and see her there again. At the next show someone said to me, "Look, Vania, Zhuchka's* there again." Finally her father grew very concerned, and to prevent an affair between his daughter and a prisoner, arranged for me to be sent to the camp on the Solovetsky Islands.

Ivan Rusinov

*Translator's note: The name "Zhuk" means beetle; the daughter was dubbed "Zhuchka" or "little beetle-girl."

Platon Nabokov with the manuscripts of poems he wrote in the prison camp. Poet, publicist, playwright and prisoner in the Ozerlag camps in Irkutsk province, Siberia, from 1951-1955. He was an actor in the camp puppet theater.

The little puppet theater was part of the camp theater at Vikhorevka, a railroad stop between Taishet and Bratsk. The prisoners worked at forestry sites and at a sawmill. The theater used to put on operettas, comedies and dramas. At my one-man puppet theater I usually staged versions of stories by Chekhov. One time I did a version of The Lion Tamer *by Sergei Obraztsov. In the final act of the play the "lion" ate up the "tamer," and then spat out his moustache. At this scene the prisoners in their dirty padded jackets laughed fit to burst, showing their toothless grins. Soon after I was summoned for interrogation to a room with a portrait of the real "Mustachioed Tamer," Joseph Stalin, on the wall. The "Godfather," i.e., the camp's investigating officer, reckoned the lion could be a symbol of British imperialism, or of Leon Trotsky. They threatened to add on a "fiver" [five-year sentence] for anti-Soviet agitation, but in the end I was only sent to a penal camp.*

Platon Nabokov

Lazar Sheryshevsky at his apartment in Moscow.

Whenever an actor went out on stage, he forgot he was a prisoner – he lived his role. But the nights in the camp were very hard. People took refuge in trying to think about the theater, about work and creativity. But the night brought thoughts of your loved ones, and of your ruined life. A day in the theater was a gilded cage, but a night in the camp barracks was a tough iron cage.

How do you feel when you act on stage for your torturers? The whole country was acting and dancing to Stalin's tune. Even before being arrested, performers were in a situation where there was no question of any creative freedom, and once they ended up in the camps, they went on serving the same system, except that now it appeared in a completely obvious and brutal form. But they were already prepared for that, already internally enslaved. The camp was a sort of Russian "matrioshka" doll – a cage within a cage.

Before his arrest, the set designer at our camp theater, my close friend Dimitr Zelenkov, worked at the famous Marynsky Theater in Leningrad. Dimitr knew that after his release from the camps, as an "enemy of the people" he wouldn't be able to live in Moscow or Leningrad. He would be condemned to wander about the provincial towns, where even if there were some sort of second-rate theaters, he still wouldn't get work in them. He often talked about this. He served eight years in the camp, and when he only had a few more months until the end of his sentence, this talented and thoroughly educated man hanged himself in the camp. He was horrified by the prospect of the life that awaited him "at liberty."

Lazar Sheryshevsky

Nina Gamilton at her apartment in Moscow.

Why did the Gulag bosses establish prison camp theaters? Purely for their own pleasure. That's all.

Nina Gamilton

EAST SIBERIAN
SEA

LAPTEV
SEA

U S S R

Anadyr

BERING
SEA

Lena

Indigirka

Kolyma

Susuma   Elgen
Yagodnoe

Chandyga

Orutukan
Ust-Omchug Magadan

Yakutsk

Okhotsk

Aldan

SEA OF
OKHOTSK

300 km

KOLYMA

KOLYMA
1931-1955

Seen from above, Kolyma is a sea of bare, rocky mountain ridges, a boundless wasteland stretching as far as the horizon. The first European to arrive was the Pole Jan Czersky, czarist exile and Siberian explorer. Towards the end of the 1920s gold was discovered in the mountains that bear his name. And that was the start of the tragedy of Kolyma.

There was only one route to the gold in the Soviet Far East: by Trans-Siberian railroad to Vladivostok, and then north by boat through the Sea of Okhotsk to Magadan on Nagaevo Bay. Between 1932 and 1957 hundreds of thousands of prisoners were brought to Kolyma by this route. The isolation and the Arctic climate made it one of the most terrible places in the Gulag.

Eduard Berzin, a Latvian who has gone down in the history of the 20th century as the organizer of the vast complex of camps at Kolyma, wanted in his youth to be a painter. Before the revolution he graduated from Berlin's Academy of Fine Arts. He met his future wife, Elza Mittenberg, also a painter, at the School of Fine Arts in Riga. They fell in love and planned to continue their studies in St. Petersburg, when Berzin was sent to the front the First World War.

At the time of the October Revolution he was commander of the First Latvian Rifle Division in the Red Army, and then fought against the Whites in the Civil War. Rather than face separation from her loved one, Elza went to the front with him. The would-be painter quickly made a career for himself in the Red Army. In 1918 his detachment guarded the train taking Lenin to Petrograd from Moscow, and Berzin was personally responsible for the security of the Leader of Revolution. He also quickly gained the trust of Feliks Dzerzhinsky and joined the Cheka, the Soviet political police. In 1928-1929 he was head of construction of a cellulose and paper combine in the Urals, where he oversaw the work of 70,000 prisoners. In 1931 Stalin personally assigned Eduard Berzin to perform a mission of strategic importance for the Soviet Union. It involved bringing the vast areas of the Kolyma River valley under economic management and mining the large gold deposits found in the region.

On February 4, 1932, the steamship *Sakhalin*, guided by an ice-breaker, smashed its way through the ice on the Sea of Okhotsk to reach port on Nagaevo Bay. There it put ashore a small group of prisoners (mainly mining engineers), a detachment of security guards and Eduard Berzin and his closest collaborators. Soon after his wife Elza and their children arrived. From his first days in Kolyma, Berzin was devoted himself entirely to work: he built the city of Magadan, founded the gold mines and set up camps for tens of thousands of prisoners.

Berzin was the czar and god of Kolyma. As head of Dalstroi, the enterprise established to manage the Soviet Far East, he had unlimited power over vast tracts of northeastern Siberia.

He single-handedly represented virtually all the branches of Soviet power: the party, the executive, the prosecution, the judiciary and the army. In exchange the Kremlin expected just one thing – as much gold as possible.

In the first year of his tenure, Berzin sent 500 kilograms of ore to Moscow, and only three years later he sent 14 metric tons. A prisoner at the Kolyma camps who was physically unable to perform 100 percent of the norm received reduced food rations, although they were meager enough to begin with. In 1933 the daily norm for extraction of gold-bearing soil was less than a cubic meter per prisoner. Two years later it was raised to two cubic meters; and in 1936, for the same ration of bread and a bowl of soup, the head of Dalstroi now demanded from four to six cubic meters a day. How many prisoners paid for that with their lives? No one knows. However, we do know that "for surpassing the mining plan" Eduard Berzin was awarded the Order of Lenin. Soon after his return from Moscow, where he received his medal from the chairman of the Supreme Council of the Soviet Union, Mikhail Kalinin, the head of Kolyma issued an order that made the situation even worse for the prisoners. From then on they would work in opencast gold mines in temperatures as low as minus 55 degrees Celsius.

In 1936 the prisoners extracted 33 metric tons of gold. That same year the Gulag received an allowance of 200 metric tons of barbed wire; 30 tons went to Dalstroi. Eduard Berzin had turned barbed wire into pure gold.

His wife Elza left a memoir, in which she described the Berzins' life in Magadan. They lived in a large villa on Berzin Street, named in his honor (now called Karl Marx Street). Fanatically devoted to the task Stalin and the Communist Party had assigned him, Eduard would spend entire days dressed in a bearskin coat, driving around the trails of Kolyma in a Rolls Royce he had been sent from Moscow, so that he could personally oversee the work in progress. He would come home late in the evening. "The children wanted to spend more time with him, but they only saw one another at breakfast and dinner. He only went hunting with Petia once; they shot three ducks and a wild goose. What a joy that was!" recalled Elza. Berzin liked music, and the couple used to listen to Tchaikovsky, Schubert and Grieg. "We had a lot of good records by the Philadelphia Orchestra that Eddie had brought back from America on an official trip in 1930." Their twelve-year-old Petia was learning to play the piano. Their fifteen-year-old daughter Mirza grew flowers in the garden next to their house, including roses, which gave her father great joy. The children performed in the school theater group run by actor-prisoners. They put on scenes from *Boris Godunov*, *Russalka* and *Eugene Onegin*.

Columns of prisoners would be marched from the port on Nagaevo Bay to the central transit camp in Magadan; their route would take them near the Berzins' house. An endless procession of inmates – tens of thousands worn out by interrogation, starvation and harassment, passed the villa with the roses. Many of them were never to return from the icy hell of the Kolyma camps.

Elza wrote in her memoirs, "It was better for the children in Magadan than in Moscow, because they had lots of fresh air and space. On the whole one can live quite well in the north…"

The Berzins spent their first holiday in Italy, visiting Rome, Venice and Sorrento, and enjoying Italian art and architecture. On the way back they stopped off in Paris and Berlin.

Soon after, the head of Dalstroi was arrested. He was accused of spying for Britain and Germany and of creating a "counterrevolutionary Trotskyite espionage and sabotage organization aiming to give Japan control of the rich gold deposits at Kolyma". On August 1, 1938, in Moscow's Lubianka prison Eduard Berzin was sentenced to death. That same day he was executed with a shot in the back of the head. Such was the logic of the Great Purge. Stalin's machine of terror had also engulfed the old Leninist cadres of Bolsheviks. The subsequent fate of the Berzin family was tragic. As the wife of "an enemy of the people" Elza spent 10 years in the camps. Petia went from an orphanage to the front and was killed at Stalingrad. Mirza was brought up by her grandmother.

Today in Magadan's central square, opposite municipal offices stands a bronze bust of Eduard Berzin. The monument was erected in 1989 on the 50th anniversary of the granting of a municipal charter to Magadan. The guest of honor at the unveiling ceremony was the granddaughter of the head of Dalstroi, Asia Odinets, Mirza's daughter. An elementary school and one of the city's main streets also bear the name of the founder of the Kolyma prisons, the biggest network of camps in the Soviet Union. However, it would be no use looking for a street or a school in Magadan named after Varlam Shalamov, the writer who spent 17 years in the Kolyma camps and wrote *Kolyma Tales*, one of the most important literary testimonies to the Gulag.

On a hill above the city stands a monument to the victims of Kolyma. A sculpture of human faces, about a dozen meters high, points north, the direction taken by the convoys of prisoners. The monument to the victims stands above the city, and the monument to the criminal in its center. Both were erected at more or less the same time.

Delivering supplies on the frozen Yana River, northwestern Kolyma.

In the first year, over 10,000 prisoners were brought to Kolyma. Their first task was to build a port on the Sea of Okhotsk and the city of Magadan – an essential supply base for development of the mining industry on the vast territory of Kolyma.

Transporting goods by reindeer-drawn sled. The opencast gold mines were located several hundred kilometers away from Magadan in roadless mountain terrain. In the 1930s supplies and equipment were transported in the summer by pack horses and floated along the rivers, and in the winter, on sleds drawn by dogs or reindeer. In the winter months a food caravan reached the Central Kolyma camps in 25-50 days, depending on the weather. A pair of draft reindeer delivered a load of 100 kilograms, and a team of 10 dogs, 100-150 kilograms. In 1936 Dalstroi had 5,300 horses, 4,500 reindeer and 900 dogs for this purpose.

Stills from a propaganda film about Kolyma, shot during the 1930s.

а/з Зимчик „Полярный"
пос. БАТАМАЙ
13/IV – 51 г.

A caterpillar tractor clearing the way to Omsukchan. Eastern Kolyma, 1950.

A vehicle buried in snow on the Tumara River on its way to the village of Ege-Khayya on the Yana River, headquarters of the Yanlag Yana Labor Camp administration. Northeastern Yakutia, 1951.

Workers at the shipping base in the village of Batamay on the winter route Polarny. Northeastern Yakutia, 1951.

Reindeer-drawn sleds on the route from Ust-Nera to Ege-Khayya. Northeastern Yakutia, 1951.

Vehicles on the route from Evgekinot to Yultin. Chukhotka, 1950.

Building a bridge over the Kolyma River, 1930s. In the 1930s Dalstroi's most important task was to build roads. In the first few years only about 15 per cent of the total number of prisoners worked in the mining sector. The rest built roads and basic infrastructure. All the work was done manually.

A camp guards' patrol, 1930s. As the prison
camp system expanded, so did the number of
escaped prisoners. In 1937 Dalstroi's operational
division for combating escapes numbered over
500 mounted riflemen and 60 soldiers with dogs.

A brigade of prisoners,
1930s. All Dalstroi's
economic activities
required a large number
of workers. In the 1930s
prisoners represented
90 per cent of the total
workforce.

The Chelbania gold mine, 1943.

Prisoners working at a gold mine,
circa 1943.

Prisoners rinsing gold in a *butar*, 1938.
The gold was rinsed in three ways:
manually, on riverbanks and in streams;
in *butary*, wooden troughs into which the
current of a stream was diverted; and
mechanically, in rinsing drums powered
by portable steam generators.

Opencast gold mines, 1938. From left to right: Rinsing gold. Drying ore-bearing soil. Opencast mining. Collecting rinsed gold.

A tin and uranium mine, Butugychag Mountains, southwestern Kolyma, turn of the 1940s and 1950s.

In 1948 the mining and enrichment of uranium ore began at Kolyma. The work was top secret. The prisoners did not know what they were mining and were not protected from radiation.

The Kolyma Route, 1938.
Inmates spent eight years
building the Kolyma Highway – a
network of roads linking
Magadan and the gold-bearing
regions of central and
southwestern Kolyma.

A store, with a sign reading *Kolymsnab*, short for *Kolymskove snabzhenie*, meaning "Kolyma Supplies." Magadan, 1943.

First of May parade. The portraits in the foreground show, from left to right: Nikita Khrushchev, Viacheslav Molotov, Anastasy Mikoian; and in the background: Andrei Zhdanov, Lavrenty Beria and Mikhail Kalinin. Magadan, 1943.

In the early 1940s Magadan was a city of 30,000, inhabited mainly by free workers who came to Kolyma in search of high salaries. Some of the citizens were prisoners who, after serving their sentences, were not allowed to leave and settled in Kolyma.

Eduard and Elza Berzin
before leaving for Kolyma.
Moscow, 1931.

Eduard Berzin and his
daughter, Mirza, a few months
before his arrest. Magadan,
spring 1937.

Eduard Berzin and his son, Petia. Magadan, spring 1937.

Elza Berzin at
Kolyma, 1930s.

Eduard Berzin, born 1894, Latvian communist, founder of the Kolyma prison camps. In 1932-1937 he was head of Dalstroi. During the Great Purge he was arrested, sentenced to death and shot in 1938 in Moscow.

At Kolyma Eduard Berzin drove a Rolls Royce that he was sent from Moscow. This car had earlier been used by Lenin's widow, Nadezhda Krupskaia.

331

KOLYMA
Historical note

The complex of camps at Kolyma was the biggest prison camp system in the USSR. It was established in 1932 to mine gold deposits in the upper and central parts of the Kolyma River and to bring the northeastern areas of the Soviet Union under economic management. At first it covered an area corresponding to today's Magadan province, then it was systematically extended, taking in the Chukotsk Peninsula, part of Yakutia, Khabarovsk Krai and Kamchatka – in total about 10 per cent of the territory of the USSR. Given the arctic climate and severe winters lasting several months, with temperatures falling to minus 65 degrees Celsius, the months of perpetual darkness, and the distance from the European part of the Soviet Union, the conditions prevailing in the Kolyma camps were exceptionally harsh.

The Kolyma prison camp network and Dalstroi, the vast, multi-branched enterprise incorporated into it, were part of the USSR camp-industrial complex that emerged in the 1930s and was one of the most important structures in the state's economy until the mid-1950s.

Prisoners at the Kolyma camps did the following work:
- prospected for and mined gold deposits in the Kolyma and Indigirka River valleys
- mined in the following Mining-Industrial Administrations: Northern, Southern, Southwestern, Western, Tenkinsky, Chai-Uriatsky and Indygirsky – in total over a dozen opencast gold mines and pits
- built and operated gold prospecting plants
- prospected for and mined over 30 tin deposits in the Kolyma, Yana and Indigirka river valleys and in Chukhotka
- prospected for and mined wolfram and molybdenum deposits
- mined cobalt and built the Upper Seimchan molybdenum smelters
- prospected for, mined and enriched radioactive raw materials from the Severny, Butugychasky, Sugunsky and other deposits
- mined coal in the regions of: Arkagala, Elgen, Zyrian and Omsukchan
- built and operated ports on the following bays: Nagaevo, Vanino, Muchka and Vesolaya, and at Pevek and Krest Bay in Chukhotka
- put up apartment and municipal buildings in Magadan and other villages and towns; constructed prison camps and camp administration buildings
- built the Kolyma Highway from Magadan to the gold-mining sites, the Madadan Highway to Yakutsk (1,850 kilometers), as well as local roads, totalling over 3,000 kilometers
- built airports at Magadan, Pevek, on the lower Indygirka, and in other places

- built a narrow-gauge railroad from Magadan to Palatka
- built and operated more than a dozen thermal and hydro-electric stations at the sources of Jack London Lake and on the Kiuelsena River
- built the following industrial power lines: Yagodnoe–Berelokh–Arkagala; Kiuelsena–Yagodny; Krest Bay–Yultin; Arkagala–Ust-Nera and others
- worked in the Kolyma River Transport Administration, the Kolyma-Indigirka and Yana River Navigation, and built a shipyard on the Kolyma River
- built and operated auxiliary enterprises, including cement plants, glass plants, brickyards, steel foundries and others
- worked in farming and forestry.

Data previously issued on the prisoner mortality rate are incomplete. For example, we know that in 1946, when there were 73,060 prisoners in Dalstroi camps, the mortality rate was 7.2 per cent, or 5,260 victims in one year. The main cause of death was malnutrition and exhausting physical work in extreme climatic conditions. During the Great Purge in 1937-1938 about 12,000 people were shot at Kolyma.

In the second half of the 1950s most of the camps were closed down, but some of them still existed in the 1960s. The date of the final closure of the Kolyma camps is unknown, because documents relating to the period after January 25, 1960 have not yet been made public. We do know that in the 1970s Kolyma was still a place of exile for political prisoners.

Chronology

1916
The presence of gold in the Sredniekan River valley in the upper basin of the Kolyma River is first mentioned.

1928
Rich gold deposits are discovered on Bezimenny Stream, a tributary of the Sredniekan River, by private prospector F. Polikarpov. Gold fever hits Okhotsk, despite an official ban and about 200-300 people go to the Sredniekan Valley, 500 kilometers away. The state enterprise Soiuzzoloto takes over the newly discovered gold-bearing region, and orders individual prospectors to hand over ore "for the set price of 1 ruble and 13 kopecks per gram." A ban is imposed on prospecting by private individuals.
The First Kolyma Geological Expedition (led by Yury Bilibin) arrives from Moscow and starts work.

1929

Yury Bilibin's geologists and Sergei Obruchev, leader of the Geological Expedition organized by the Yakutsk Branch of the USSR Academy of Sciences, announce that the Czerski Mountain range in the upper Kolyma River valley is a huge gold-bearing area, 700 kilometers long and 150-200 kilometers wide.

The Soiuzzoloto's opencast gold mines do not have enough equipment.

Fall: mining is suspended because of famine in the Sredniekan region.

Eighty-nine kilograms of gold are extracted.

1930

The First Kolyma Geological Expedition continues work.

Two hundred and seventy-four kilograms of gold are extracted.

1931

November 13: a decree of the USSR Labor and Defense Council establishes the State Company for Roadworks and Industrial Construction in the Upper Kolyma Region to be known as Dalstroi (short for Far East Construction Project). Its purpose is to bring the northern part of the USSR Far East under economic management, and above all to prospect for and mine gold deposits in the upper and central parts of the Kolyma River and its tributaries (a total area of about 400,000 square kilometers).

Dalstroi is placed under the direct command of the USSR Labor and Defense Council; allocated capital for its start-up period totaling 300 million rubles and exempted from all taxes and duties.

Eduard Berzin is appointed managing director of Dalstroi.

Fall: all work at Soiuzzoloto's opencast gold mines is suspended because of famine.

One hundred and fifty-three kilograms of gold are extracted.

1932

In December the number of prisoners is 11,100.

Ten percent of all prisoners work in the mining sector.

February 4: Eduard Berzin, the managers of Dalstroi and the first small group of prisoners, mining industry experts, arrive from Vladisvostok on board the *Sakhalin* and depart for the village of Nagaevo on the Sea of Okhotsk.

April 1: the Northeastern Corrective Labor Camps, or Sevvostlag, are established and overseen by the head of Dalstroi.

Radion Vashkov is appointed head of Sevvostlag.

October: a resolution is passed by the Central Committee of the All-Union Communist Party (Bolshevik) defining the area of Dalstroi's activities as a separate administrative territory belonging to the Fareastern Krai.

Prisoners are imported in large numbers.

Building starts on the port on Nagaevo Bay and the settlement of Magadan.

Soiuzzoloto is closed down.

Five hundred kilograms of gold are extracted.

1933

In December the number of prisoners is 27,390.

The number of free workers is 3,392.

Dalstroi's basic infrastructure is constructed. Eighty-five per cent of all prisoners are put to work building roads, the settlement of Magadan and the camps.

Eight hundred kilograms of gold are extracted.

1934

On January 1, the number of prisoners is 29,659.

Captain of State Security I. G. Filipov is appointed head of Sevvostlag.

Infrastructure construction continues. Gold mining starts on an industrial scale.

The number of prisoners working in mining increases to 22 per cent.

The daily norm for extraction of gold-bearing soil by each prisoner is raised from 0.8 to 2 cubic meters.

Five and a half tons of gold are extracted.

1935

On January 1, the number of prisoners is 36,313.

The daily norm for extraction of gold-bearing soil by each prisoner is raised to 4-6 cubic meters.

Fourteen tons of gold are extracted.

1936

On January 1, the number of prisoners is 48,740.

July: about 200 communists imprisoned at the transit camp in Magadan hold a hunger strike. The hunger strikers send a statement to the USSR Central Executive Committee and the NKVD demanding recognition for the status of political prisoners. About 250 inmates put up resistance during their transportation from Magadan to the Kolyma camps. Group hunger strikes are held by imprisoned communists fighting for the status of political prisoners at various Kolyma camps.

An order is issued by the USSR People's Council of Commissars to extend geological prospecting to the Indygirka River valley in northern Yakutia, thereby increasing Dalstroi's territory to a total of 700,000 square kilometers.

Thirty-three tons of gold are extracted.

1937

On January 1, the number of prisoners is 70,414.

Thirty percent of all prisoners work in the mining sector.

Spring–fall: group trials are held for communists who had fought for the status of political prisoners the year before. At least 85 people are shot. There is a mass influx of prisoners sentenced under political articles in connection with the Great Purge.

August 4: the writer Varlam Shalamov arrives at Magadan with a consignment of prisoners; he will spend 17 years in the Kolyma prison camps.

December 2: a group of NKVD officials from Moscow arrives at Magadan on board the *Nikolai Ezhov* (including K. A. Pavlov, S. N. Garanin, and prosecutor L. P. Metelev), who are to replace Eduard Berzin and other managers of Dalstroi and Sevvostlag.

December 17: the head of Sevvostlag, Captain of State Security I. G. Filipov, is arrested in Magadan and later shot.

December 19: Eduard Berzin is arrested on his way to Moscow for a holiday.

Senior Major of State Security Karp Pavlov takes over as head of Dalstroi.

Colonel Stepan Garanin takes over as head of Sevvostlag.

The camp regime is made more rigorous, with a 12-hour work day and a reduction in food rations.

Fifty-one tons of gold are extracted.

1938

On January 1, the number of prisoners is 90,741.

Forty-seven percent of all prisoners work in the mining sector.

March 4: a decree issued by the USSR People's Council of Commissars places Dalstroi under NKVD administration. Its name is changed to Chief Administration for Far North Construction, or GUSDS Dalstroi.

Karp Pavlov announces a campaign labeled "All hands to the mines."

Prisoners are transferred from other Dalstroi departments to the gold mines without any infrastructure being made ready for them, which causes a sharp rise in the mortality rate.

June 11: the head of Dalstroi issues an order making it possible to extend a prisoner's work day to 16 hours.

Prisoners and free workers at Dalstroi are arrested and interrogated. Those arrested are beaten and tortured to force false confessions.

Death sentences are issued in large numbers by an NKVD troika, consisting of chairman Senior Lieutenant of State Security Vasily Speransky and members Captain of State Security M. P. Kononovich and prosecutor L.P. Metelyev. Mass executions take place at the opencast gold mines in all the mining regions of Dalstroi and at the Serpantinka special camp, near the headquarters of the Northern Administration at Khattyny.

There is a further mass influx of political prisoners, victims of the Great Purge, replacing those who have perished or been shot. (Conditions were terrible in the overcrowded camps. 100-120 people were packed into tents and blocks designed to house 40-50 prisoners; canteens designed for 100 had to feed 2,000-2,500; and meals were served outside through hatches in temperatures of minus 40-50 degrees celsius.)

August 1: Eduard Berzin is executed in a Moscow prison.

September: Sevvostlag head Colonel Stepan Garanin is arrested on a charge of spying for Japan (he will die in the Pechora Labor Camps in 1950).

Sixty-two tons of gold are extracted.

1939

On January 1, the number of prisoners is 138,170.

Commissar of State Security Rank III Lieutenant General Ivan Nikishov is appointed head of Dalstroi.

Captain of State Security A. A. Vishnevetsky is appointed head of Sevvostlag.

Magadan is granted a municipal charter.

October 11: the writer Evgenia Ginzburg arrives at Magadan with a consignment of prisoners; she will spend 18 years in the camps.

Sixty-six tons of gold are extracted.

1940

On January 1, the number of prisoners is 190,309.

There is no data on the amount of gold extracted.

1941-1944

On January 1, the number of prisoners is:

1941: 187,976		1943: 107,755	
1942: 177,775		1944: 84,716	

In 1941 the number of prisoners working in the mining industry reaches 79 per cent of the total.

March 19, 1941: a decree is issued by the USSR People's Council of Commissars adding part of the coast of the Sea of Okhotsk and the Yana River basin in the Republic of Yakutia to Dalstroi's territory, giving it a total area of 2,266,000 square kilometers.

May 1941: Battalion Commissar (later Colonel of State Security) Y. I. Drabkin is appointed head of Sevvostlag.

During the Second World War, Dalstroi is the main supplier of tin and wolfram ore for the arms industry.

Transports of food and supplies reaching Kolyma are reduced.

Work norms are increased; 16-hour work days are introduced and food rations are lowered. Prisoners who have completed their sentences are detained in the camps until the end of the war.

June 1944: US Vice President Henry Wallace and US Military Information Department representative Professor Owen Lattimor visit Kolyma on their way from Alaska to China. They have a meeting with the head of Dalstroi, Ivan Nikishov. A special show is performed for the guests at USSR NKVD Dalstroi's Gorky Theater of Music and Drama.

(The Dalstroi authorities carefully organized the Americans' visit so that they would never guess the camps existed. Professor Lattimor later wrote that "Mr and Mrs Nikishov are distinct for their deep awareness of civic responsibility. The economic management of the northern areas of the USSR is run according to a plan, and the entirety of the work is organized by the marvelous Dalstroi, which can be compared to America's Hudson Bay Company.")

1944: the number of free workers at Dalstroi exceeds the number of prisoners for the first time and totals about 92,000.

The annual average amount of gold extracted is 45 tons.

1945

On January 1, the number of prisoners is 93,542.

Major General N. F. Titov is appointed head of Sevvostlag.

An amnesty involving criminal prisoners is announced to mark the end of the war.

There is an influx of arrested representatives of national movements from Ukraine and the Baltic Republics, Poles, Hungarians, Romanians, Czechs, Germans and Japanese, as well as former Soviet prisoners-of-war and people forcibly deported to do labor in Germany, who are accused of betraying the fatherland.

From 1945, figures for the amount of gold extracted are kept secret.

1946

On January 1, the number of prisoners is 73,060.

1947

On January 1, the number of prisoners is 93,322.

1948

On January 1, the number of prisoners is 106,893.

Major General I. G. Petrenko is appointed head of Dalstroi.

Major General A. A. Derevianenko is appointed head of Sevvostlag.

February 28: the MVD issues an order creating Special Camp No. 5 or Berlag. Absorbing some of the Sevvostlag camps, it is designed for political prisoners serving long sentences, where a more rigorous regime similar to that of a prison is in force, and the prisoners are used for particularly tough jobs.

Uranium ore extraction begins at Kolyma.

1949

On January 1, the number of prisoners is 108,865.

On October 1, 1949, the largest groups of prisoners in *Sevvostlag* by nationality are (in total the document lists 31 nationalities):

Russian:	61,4 %	Tatars:	1,8 %
Ukranians:	18 %	Germans:	1,1 %
Belarussians:	4,2 %	Polish:	less than 1 %

(Poles from Eastern territories of prewar Poland, annexed by the USSR, were treated as Soviet citizens).

The camp for Japanese prisoners-of-war, totaling 3,479, is closed down.

1950

On January 1, the number of prisoners is 153,317.

Director General of Mining Rank Two I. L. Mitrakov is appointed head of Dalstroi.

1951

The number of prisoners is 182,958.

Dalstroi's territory is increased to 3 million square kilometers by a decree of the presidium of the USSR Supreme Council on the basis of a proposal made by the MVD.

1952

On January 1, the number of prisoners is 199,726.

1953

On January 1, the number of prisoners is 175,078.

March 5: Stalin dies.

March 18: in accordance with a decree issued by the USSR Council of Ministers, the Chief Administration for Far North Construction Dalstroi is transferred to the administration of the USSR Ministry of Metallurgy.

March 27: a decree is issued by the USSR Supreme Council announcing an amnesty, which in practice does not include political prisoners. A large number of criminal prisoners are released from the camps. There is a distinct improvement in conditions at the camps.

September: a new Northeastern Corrective Labor Camps Administration, USVITL, is created, with I. Mitrakov as head.

1954

On January 1, the number of prisoners is 88,077.

Special Camp No. 5, known as Berlag, is closed and all camp units are transferred to the Northeastern Corrective Labor Camps Administration, USVITL.

1955

On January 1, the number of prisoners is 72,177.

A decree by the USSR government permits most of the Poles in the USSR, including those imprisoned in the camps, to depart for Poland.

1956

On January 1, the number of prisoners is 39,645.

Colonel D. Lubenchenko is appointed head of Northeastern Corrective Labor Camps Administration, *USVITL.*

1957

On January 1, the number of prisoners is 23,890.

April 16: the Ministry of Internal Affairs issues a decree to start closing down the Northeastern Corrective Labor Camps Administration, *USVITL.*

1958

July: the Northeastern Corrective Labor Camps Administration, *USVITL,* closes down completely.

Sources :

1. Malgorzata Gizejewska, "Poles at Kolyma, 1940-1943", published by PAN ISP, Warsaw 1997.

2. Malgorzata Gizejewska, *Kolyma 1944-1956 we wspomnieniach polskich wiezniów* ["Kolyma 1944-1956 in the memoirs of Polish prisoners"], published by PAN ISP, Warsaw 2000.

3. Alexandr Kozlov, *Iz istorii kolymskikh lagerei (1932-1937)* ["From the history of the Kolyma camps (1932-1937)"], in the almanac. *Kraevedcheskie Zapiski* ["Local History Notes"] No. XVII, Magadanskoe knizhnoe izdatelstvo, Magadan 1991.

4. Alexandr Kozlov, *Iz istorii kolymskikh lagerei (1932-1937)* ["From the history of the Kolyma camps (1932-1937)"], in the almanac. *Kraevedcheskie Zapiski* ["Local History Notes"] No. XIX, *Magadanskoe knizhnoe izdatelstvo,* Magadan 1993.

5. Alexandr Kozlov, Magadan. *Konspekt proshlogo* ["Magadan. A Summary of the past"], Magadanskoe knizhnoe izdatelstvo, Magadan 1990.

6. Alexandr Navasardov, *Iz istorii razvitia transporta na Kolymye (1931-1940)* ["From the history of the development of transportation in Kolyma (1931-1940)"], in the almanac. *Kraevedcheskie zapiski* ["Local History Notes"] No. XV, Magadanskoye knizhnoye izdatelstvo, Magadan 1988.

7. Nina Savoeva, *Mesto naznachenia – Magadan* ["Destination – Magadan"]. *Meditsinsky Biulleten* ["Medical Bulletin"] No. 31, Magadanskoye knizhnoe izdatelstvo, Magadan 1991.

8. Sergei Sigachev, ["Chief Administration of Far North Construction", "Northeastern Corrective Labor Camp Administration", "Northeastern Corrective Labor Camps"] in ["The Prison Camps. An Encyclopedic Guide"], issued by the Memorial Center for Research, Information and Dissemination (NIPC) in Moscow, jointly edited by Nikita Okhotin and Arseny Roginsky.

9. Tamara Smolina, *Sudba Berzynikh* ["The Fate of the Berzins"], in the monthly *Na Severe Dalnem* ["In the Far North"], February 1988.

A day in the camp was like this: reveille at 5 a.m. was accompanied by insistent banging against a rail by the gate and shouting – a stream of obscene abuse from the camp staff aimed at the laggards. Anyone who overslept was pulled by the feet from their bunk to the floor. There were always some corpses among them. Then came breakfast in the packed canteen, which meant wolfing it down while looking around you for fear of anyone trying to take away your "dream meal" (bread and hot water). Then they banged the rail again to call everyone outside before the gate. At the gate there was an indescribable crush and commotion. Prisoners were beaten, pushed and slapped, put into ranks for work brigades and counted, then shoved out of the gate. Before them lay 12 hours of crushingly hard work.

When I spent a few months working at the repair shop on the Central Highway, every day I saw lines of sleds full of victims from the mining camps. The sleds moved slowly along the Orotukan riverbed to the Northern Mining Administration hospital. The skin-covered skeletons lay without moving, in uncomfortable positions, even one on top of another, just as they had been arranged. Their faces were livid, with seeping wounds from frostbite. Their eyes, motionless and glassy, had no expression and gave no reaction – they were the dead eyes of people who were still alive.

Walenty Woronowicz, prisoner at the Kolyma camps, 1937-1955

There was a general view that if you survived a year at Kolyma, you could probably survive anything. That first year was terrible. What I remember from that time is constant hunger, being surrounded on all sides by a cloud of snow, frost ringing in my ears, being emaciated and expecting to die. The night cast a tight shroud over the earth. The cold penetrated to your bones, and you were enveloped in an overwhelming desire to fall asleep and disconnect yourself from reality. If I close my eyes I can see the endless night illuminated by the white glow of the snow.

I was in a work gang that carried ore from the mines to the rinsing site in wheelbarrows. During one shift each of us had to take out 120 wheelbarrows. I was already a real "dokhodiaga" [a goner], on the edge of final exhaustion. I couldn't move that many wheelbarrows, but the gang leader was relentless. (...) I'd fail to achieve the norm, get less food and feel worse and worse, but I still went on summoning up the effort and shifting those wheelbarrows. (...) The frosts had started again. Once I found an extinguished bonfire, gathered up the ashes and lay down on them. I curled up and covered myself with a wheelbarrow, I wanted to live, to survive. When it was time to go back to the camp, they couldn't find me. A man's missing! He's escaped! Finally they found me and I was beaten so badly that I couldn't get up. The other prisoners dragged me back to the camp.

Janusz Siemiński

We worked at a forestry site. We had to fell a tree, chop off the branches, cut it into two-meter pieces and pile them in cords. Some of the trees, after cutting off their tops, had to be carried to a more accessible spot, from where a tractor collected them. Several women carried huge logs on their shoulders, often for several kilometers. In winter, when wood was needed not just for fuel but also to keep the power station going, it was carried several kilometers by sled. And it was we who had to pull the sleds uphill, then, once they were loaded, bring them down a steep hill at a run, holding them back so they wouldn't get broken. It was a monstrous effort, and we weren't taken back to the camp until we had completed a very large norm. We quite often returned just at reveille, were fed a penalty ration of bread and tea and driven straight back to the forest.

Irena Krajewska, prisoner at the Kolyma camps, 1946-1954

Sources :

Irena Krajewska, *Sila nadziei* ["The Strength of Hope"], in the independent historical quarterly *Karta*, no. 1/1991.

Janusz Siemiński, *Moja Kolyma* ["My Kolyma"], *Karta*, Warsaw 1995.

Walenty Woronowicz, *Przypadki XX wieku* ["Events of the Twentieth Century"], Warsaw 1994.

KOLYMA
Memories

Decommissioned line of the narrow-gauge mountain railroad that led to the tin and uranium mines, built by prisoners in 1937-1954. Butugychag Mountains, southwestern Kolyma.

Decommissioned tin and uranium mines in the Butugychag Mountain Range.

Vestiges of tin and uranium mines.

Prisoners' shoes near the former Tsentralny camp in the valley of the Terrasovy River. The camps in the Butugychag region accommodated almost exclusively political prisoners sentenced to the most severe punishment.

A children's swing near the home of the commandant of Sopka camp, Captain Andrei Maleev, who lived with his wife and children in a house situated above the camp. On the steep hillside in the spot where the house once stood are the remains of a stove, a rusty bed and the children's swing. It was built by prisoners from thick wooden beams and steel bars – materials available in the mine. The swing stood on the edge of a stone terrace, so that the child could see the camp below him: the roofs of the barracks, the barbed wire and the prisoners. The Sopka camp was the worst camp in Butugychag. Set high in the mountains, on bare rocky slopes, in the winter it was exposed to icy hurricane-strong winds and in the summer it lacked water.

This camp had the highest mortality rate among prisoners. If they hadn't taken me to another camp in Lower Butugychag I'd never have survived.
                    Valery Ladeishchikov, a prisoner at
                        the Kolyma camps, 1945-1954.

Remains of the isolation cell in the Terrasovy River valley, Butugychag Mountain Range. A prisoner sentenced to the isolation cell served his punishment in his underwear alone, in a cell with no bed and a cement or stone floor. The guard gave him a plank to sleep on for the night. The daily food ration consisted of 300 grams of bread and a glass of hot water, and every third day a quarter of a liter of warm soup. Sentences in the isolation cell, solitary or group, with or without work duty could last for two weeks. There are well-known accounts by former prisoners that tell of frequent incidents of cruelty, such as imprisonment in a cell with no windows, or being doused with water in below-freezing temperatures.

The ruins of Sopka camp.

The bust of Eduard Berzin in front
of the municipal offices on Maxim
Gorky Square in Magadan.

Magadan. A house on Eduard Berzin Street, and
in the background, on the hill, the monument to
victims of the Kolyma camps.

Lenin Square in Magadan. In the center is the unfinished headquarters of the Soviet Communist Party. Construction was suspended in 1989 for lack of money shortly before the communist system in Russia collapsed.

An opencast gold mine in Dzhelgala
Valley in the Yagodzhinsky region.

Warming up a frozen *butar*,
a simple device for rinsing gold.

The opencast gold mine in the Dzhelgala Valley in the Yagodzhinsky region. Just as in Stalinist times, gold mining is done by opencast methods. Bulldozers tear open the surface layer of earth and shovel it into *butary* – simple devices for rinsing gold.

The village of Yagodnoe – in
Stalinist times the headquarters
of Dalstroi's Northern Corrective
Labor Camp Administration,
which was in charge of the
camps working for the Central
Kolyma gold mines.

A decommissioned uranium
enrichment plant in the
Terrasovy River valley,
Butugychag Mountains,
southwestern Kolyma.

At the enrichment plant, uranium concentrate was gathered like this: the prisoners opened centrifuges about 14 meters in diameter and extracted a sticky substance similar to thick soap, and then dried it in rust-proof baths. The dried concentrate was carried by hand into a tunnel in the hillside, where it was weighed into 16-kilogram portions and packed into special bags similar to postal sacks, with lead seals at the corners. Above the entrance to the tunnel was an armored gun site for two heavy machine guns, surrounded by barbed wire. Guards were permanently stationed at this site. The entrance was closed by a grating made from railroad tracks, and further on there was an armor-plated wall with two machine guns, one on the left and the other on the right. When a large amount of uranium concentrate had been gathered in the tunnel a so-called "escort" drove up. At its head was a jeep, behind that an armored car with a machine gun, a truck with soldiers and a lorry with an armor-plated crate, into
which the concentrate was loaded. At the back of the column there was yet another lorry with soldiers, and a jeep.

Piotr Khmelnitsky, a prisoner at the Butugychag camps.

THE BLACK MAMA

Nina Savoeva came to Kolyma of her own free will after completing her medical studies in 1940. For the next 12 years she was a doctor in the camp hospitals. She got her first job in the camp at the Chkalov gold mine in Ust-Urye.

What I saw was terrible. They quite often removed corpses that were already stiff from the vehicles that brought new consignments of prisoners to the Chkalov mine. The political prisoners sentenced under Article 58, who were the majority, were very much weakened and exhausted. In the winter pneumonia was rampant, and in the summer dysentery. The accommodation blocks in the camps were poorly insulated and badly heated. The prisoners were dressed and shod in worn out camp rags. The food was poor and low in calories, and on top of that those meager food rations were shamelessly stolen on the way from the store to the camp canteen. In the winter there wasn't enough wood for fuel or enough drinking water. It was made from melted snow. The entire camp was infested with lice. The areas for disinfecting clothes were ineffective – the lice stayed alive, and the clothes were given back damp, so people went to work in them in minus 50 degrees for at least a dozen hours. Almost every day dead prisoners were brought to the hospital, or taken straight to the morgue. They died on the spot in the gold mines from emaciation or hypothermia. Frostbite was a universal, common occurrence. In the infirmary frostbitten fingers and toes were amputated routinely – every day a bowl was filled with them.

My first acquaintance with the gold mine and camp life taught me to understand two things. First, no one was interested in saving the lives of these unfortunate people, whose main "illnesses" were hunger and emaciation. Second, within this system the only service that was not hostile to the prisoners was the medical service –with all its limitations on rights and possibilities. I tried to make sure that my next 12 years as a camp doctor would be based on understanding these two fundamental things.

I wrote reports to all levels of authority, even to the head of Dalstroi himself, General Ivan Nikishov, but with no result. The camp heads and guards regarded my behavior with hostility and amazement. The head of the camp guard, Yurchenko, once said to me, "Aren't you a bit over-concerned about the enemies of our people and our fatherland? Watch out in case it ends badly for you."

From the memoirs of Nina V. Savoeva, "Mesto naznachenia – Magadan." ("Destination Magadan"). Mieditsinksy Buletin, no. 31. Magadan 1991.

Nina Savoeva and Boris Leshniak at their apartment in Moscow.

Taking advantage of her position as director of the camp hospitals and as a member of the Soviet Communist Party, Nina Savoeva with great determination and energy acted on behalf of the prisoners, often coming into sharp conflict with the camp administration, for which she herself was very nearly arrested. The prisoners called her "Black Mama" because of her appearance – she was an Ossetian. Her renown even reached the most distant camps in Kolyma. Among the prisoners it was a known fact that "Black Mama's" hospital meant salvation.

At the Central Hospital of Northern Corrective Labor Camp Administration Dalstroi in the village of Belichie near the town of Yagodnoe, Nina Savoeva met Boris Leshniak, who was serving a 10-year sentence for, among other things, possessing the poetry of Nikolai Gumilev and Anna Akhmatova. Boris Leshniak worked in the hospital as a paramedic. Together they saved many lives.

As Varlam Shalamov wrote in *Kolyma Tales*, "We knew we could survive only by accident." The accident that may have saved his life was that, when extremely emaciated, he ended up in the hospital at Belichie. Nina Savoeva and Boris Leshniak realized that Varlam Shalamov, as a sensitive, talented man, was condemned to a quick death in the camp. After treating him, Black Mama found him a job in the hospital to protect him from murderous physical labor in the gold mines. The writer Evgenia Ginzburg also spent a long time in Belichiye under Nina Savoeva's care, and later described her camp experiences in her famous memoir.

After serving his sentence and being released from the camp, Boris Leshniak was not allowed to leave for Moscow. Nina Savoeva stayed with him at Kolyma, they continued working in the camp hospitals. They were married in Magadan in 1946. Then, because she had married a former prisoner, Nina Savoeva was expelled from the Communist Party. They had a daughter, who is now a piano instructor at the music school in Magadan. After retiring in 1972, Nina Savoeva and Boris Leshniak moved to Moscow.

Remains of the Central
Hospital of Northern
Corrective Labor Camp
Administration Dalstroi in
the village of Belichie near
Yagodnoe.

Anna Dzhenkiv, a Ukrainian,
former prisoner at the Sopka
and Vakhanka camps in the
Butugychag Mountain range
in front of her home in Ust-
Omchug, southwestern Kolyma.

Wladyslaw Chrystuk, Polish Captain in the Home Army, arrested by the NKVD in 1944 in Lida,
sentenced to five years and deported to Kolyma. In the camp he worked at forestry sites and in the
gold mines. When released after serving his sentence in 1949 he was not allowed to leave Kolyma.
He married a Russian woman. He was not allowed to leave for Poland during the repatriation of Poles
from the Soviet Union in 1956. He worked at Kolyma as a carpenter for 36 years. He lives in
Yagodnoe, on Eduard Berzin Street.

Ivan Panikarov came to Kolyma from central Russia for a few years to make some money, but stayed for good. He worked as a plumber. He was stunned when he learned about the Kolyma camps from local residents. In 1991, on his own initiative, he collected some money, and with a group of friends set up an obelisk at the former site of the Serpantinka special camp near the village of Khattyny, where mass executions took place during the Great Purge.

A year later, at a time when the temperature was minus 40 degrees Celsius, the local heating plant broke down and the entire heating system in Yagodnoe froze. Ivan Panikarov spent the next year repairing the damaged radiators. With the money he earned he bought a two-room apartment and opened a private Museum in Memory of the Victims of Political Repression. In it he has a collection of remnants of Kolyma's camp history: prisoners' bowls, gloves, hats, tools, memoirs, and tapes recordings of camp songs. He has drawn up a precise map of the Central Kolyma camps, and at his own expense has written and published a book entitled *The History of the Central Kolyma Villages*. He works as a journalist at the local newspaper.

The museum is the headquarters of the Society in Memory of the Victims of Political Repression, also founded by Ivan Panikarov. The Society helps the families of former prisoners to find information about their lost relatives. For example, in the MVD archive in Magadan Panikarov discovered documents concerning the father of Vera Pykhtin, who was born in the Elgen camp in 1943. Her mother, a political prisoner, died in the camp soon after Vera's birth. The three-year-old child was adopted by a camp guard. The little girl knew nothing about her father. Ivan Panikarov established that Piotr Pykhtin was a Ukrainian sentenced to 10 years for "counterrevolutionary activity". In the summer of 1942, he came to the Elgen camp, where he met Vera's mother. In fall he was taken to the Chay-Uria camp in Yakutia, where he died a few months later.

Ivan Panikarov in the window of his private museum in the village of Yagodnoe. The inscription on the sign reads: Museum in Memory of the Victims of Political Repression (third floor, apartment 109), open from 13:00 to 16:00, Saturdays and Sundays.

Ruins of a camp in Dzhelgala
Valley, where the writer
Varlam Shalamov was
imprisoned for some time.

VORKUTA

VORKUTA

1931-1956

Two men dressed in padded jackets and earflap hats are each holding a white bird. The man on the left seems to be touching the creature in disbelief. The other man, smiling enigmatically, gazes into the distance. Both men were released from Soviet prison camps where they had spent over 11 years. The white birds, which look like doves, are arctic partridges. This picture was taken at Vorkuta above the Arctic Circle in 1956.

The man on the left is Stanislaw Kialka, a soldier of the Polish Home Army and a hero of the anti-Nazi and anti-Soviet resistance movement. He was also a close collaborator of Aleksander Krzyzanowki, commander of the Home Army's Vilnius District, who went by the pseudonym Wolf. In the resistance he worked in a cell that forged German documents. This cell also organized underground printing presses, manufactured hand-grenades and transferred weapons and between Vilnius and Warsaw. In addition, he helped the family of victims of the Nazis. Arrested by the Gestapo, he managed to escape with the help of his fellow Home Army soldiers. He was wounded during the attempted recapture of Vilnius in July 1944. He was awarded Poland's highest decorations for his work in the resistance: the Silver Cross "Virtuti Militari," the Silver Cross of Merit with Swords and the Gallantry Cross. Arrested by the NKVD in 1945, he was sentenced to 15 years of hard labor in the camps. In the Vorkutlag camps, he organized the prisoners to help one another.

The other man is Wiktor Han, a Pole from Latvia sentenced to 20 years of labor in the Vorkutlag camps.

Stalin had planned to absorb Poland into the Soviet Union, but the Home Army, which was loyal to the Polish government in London, was fighting for independence. This political enemy was ruthlessly crushed. In the final phase of the war, members of the Polish armed resistance were arrested in large numbers by the NKVD and either shot or sentenced by Soviet military tribunals to up to 25 years' imprisonment. They were sent to the furthest, most northernly camps in the Soviet Union: Vorkuta, Norilsk and Kolyma. Their families often had no idea what had happened to them or where they were. Deprived of the right to correspond and forced to do the hardest labor, they were sentenced to oblivion and a slow death in a place above the Arctic Circle. Not until Stalin's death three years later were their sentences abolished and those Polish prisoners who had managed to survive for over 10 years were set free. For them, the Second World War had lasted for not six, but sixteen years. It only ended when they came back to Poland from the camps in 1956. Most of their families thought they were dead or lost forever. There were cases of people coming back and visiting their own symbolic graves, and of others who found out that their wives had married their brothers.

Michal Horwath wrote a message to his wife Anna on a piece of fabric he had torn from his shirt. In 1945 it was smuggled out of the NKVD prison at Chorkov in Lwów disctrict. Soon after Michal Horwath was transported to the Vorkuta camps, where he had no correspondence rights.

I wrote don't know if you got it. I repeat they sentenced me to 15 years for be[ing] a member of the Home Army <u>as a Sov.[iet] citizen</u>. I appealed – with no result. You as my family must protest here and in the West against sentencing me <u>as a Sov. citizen</u>. Tell my friends about it. They didn't prove my guilt. Maybe a lawyer will help! Send me messages in dried bread rolls. I want lots of polit.[ical] papers, some tobacco – I'm not smoking. In a few days they'll take us away. Send dried bread, a clay pot (1-2 ltr) I'll send news hid[den] in pap[er] bags. Maybe Janek as a sol.[dier] can do something – I want to be judged <u>as a Polish cit.[izen]</u>. How are you, Mama and Janek? Why are you in Tarnop.[ol] Go West! I believe it'll be good. If it's hard for you, sell my things. "Peredache" [packages] for the too rich. Many thanks for your efforts. Best to you all and Ola Br. Send the Polish-Sov.[iet] treaty on resettlement of Poles from the paper dated 6 VII. 1945. Michal

After their release from the camps, the Poles waited in Vorkuta for several months until they were permitted to leave for Poland. During this time they lived in the camp barracks, which had now been converted into apartments. There they would sometimes chat, sing songs and dance. The priests — who had also been prisoners — would secretly celebrate mass and conduct wedding ceremonies. The Poles continued to work in the Vorkuta mines and factories; however, they were now paid a salary. Several of them bought cameras in Vorkuta and took souvenir pictures. This led to a unique collection of photographs that serves as a record of their salvation and return to life.

Stanislaw Kialka built his own camera while still in the camp. He made the lens out of the corrective glass found in an ordinary pair of eyeglasses. For film he used X-ray plates that another Pole, Henryk Jasinski, had taken from the hospital where he worked. That was also where they got hold of the chemicals for developing and finishing the film. Kialka took photos of his closest companions, as well as several shots of the camp. One day someone informed on him about these activities. The NKVD men searched the entire workshop where Kialka worked, but couldn't find the camera. It was hidden in a tree stump, which had an axe planted in it. The portrait of Kialka and Han holding the arctic partridges was taken with that very camera.

"Those were fine times, filled with great joy. We were longing to live normal lives," says Wanda Kialka, recalling the first weeks after their release. Wanda Kialka, born Cejko, spent over 11 years in the Vorkuta camps. Before her arrest she was a messenger and nurse with the Home Army partisan divisions. In 1944 her brother was killed, along with his entire 50-man partisan unit, which fell into an NKVD ambush. Wanda was sentenced by a Soviet military tribunal to 20 years of hard labor. Sent to Vorkuta, she worked in the mines, quarries and a tailor shop. She met Stanislaw Kialka after being released from the camp. Three years later, back in Poland, they were married.

For many years the pictures taken in Vorkuta in 1956 had to be kept under wraps. In the Communist Polish People's Republic, the authorities treated former prisoners held in Soviet camps as "politically suspect elements" and second-class citizens. Censorship was in force on anything concerning the Gulag, and bringing up the subject could lead to repressive measures by the political police. The photographs lived a secret life in the bottom of dresser drawers and private albums seen only by relatives or close friends.

One of these pictures shows a man and a woman standing on a road disappearing into the horizon. Their faces are solemn and intense. They are staring into the camera. The man is holding a cigarette. They are Jadwiga Olechnowicz and Witold Augusewicz, two other Poles released from the camps. Behind them is an empty landscape and a forest of crosses in the tundra. It became the prison cemetery for those who took part in a rebellion in the camp at Mine No. 29, which was violently suppressed by the NKVD.

In July 1953 seven of the seventeen Vorkuta camp groups went on strike. The prisoners in the camp at Mine No. 29, where Witold Augusewicz was held, also refused to go to work. The strikers demanded that their sentences be abolished and that they be set free. They took over the camp and released their comrades from the isolation cells. A strike committee consisting of Russians, Ukrainians and Poles, was set up to keep order in the camp. The protest went on for six days. On August 1, the camp was surrounded by troops. Prosecutor Roman Rudenko (Chief Soviet Prosecutor at the Nuremberg Trials) and General of Internal Forces Ivan Maslennikov personally commanded this action. When asked to leave the territory of the camp, the prisoners refused and passively resisted when the soldiers tried to drag them out one by one. Soon afterwards, the troops, positioned with machine guns in the watchtowers, opened fire on the crowd of prisoners gathered in the camp courtyard. About 70 people were killed, and 130 were wounded. Witold Augusewicz saw people dying all around him under a hail of bullets. Luckily, he managed to escape the gunfire.

The strike leaders were arrested. Only a few months earlier, when Stalin was still alive, they would have received the death penalty, but now they were sentenced to an additional 10 years. Some of the prisoners who took part in the strike were sent to penal camps, and the rest were driven out to work. Three years later most of the Poles were released, including the strike organizers and participants.

Smuggled message written on pieces of matchbox sent by Stefania Szantyr to her family from an NKVD prison in 1945. Stefania Szantyr spent 11 years in the Vorkuta camps, and returned to Poland in 1956.

Thank you very much for everything. Don't forget …

… that Stenia loves you forever.

A message for his mother that Stanislaw Krzaklewski threw out of a freight car while being transported to the Soviet camps in 1945. Three days later an unknown little girl delivered the message to the addressee.

Janina Krzaklewska. Profesorska Estate. 2 Ptasnik Street. Lwów. I'm going east alone. 4. II. 1945. I beg you mother and Jula leave for the west immediately. Stach.

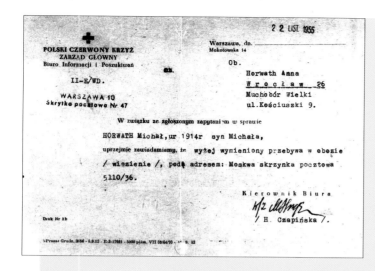

Anna Horwath tried to discover her husband's fate through the Polish Red Cross, but her efforts went unanswered. The first indication that Michal Horwath was alive came only in November 1955, 10 years after she received his message smuggled out of the prison. In 1956 Michal Horwath returned to Poland.

Polish Red Cross, Chief Administration, Office of Information and Inquiries.
14 Mokotowska Street, Warsaw, November 22, 1955
Citizen Anna Horwath, 9 Kosciuszko Street, Muchobór Wielki, Wroclaw 26.
Regarding the question you submitted concerning Michal Horwath, born 1914, son of Michal, we wish to inform you that the above-named person is in a camp (prison) at the following address: PO Box 5110/36, Moscow

Bureau Chief
H. Czapińska

Witold Augusewicz and Jadwiga Olechnowicz, who had spent 10 years in the camps, met after being set free. Their marriage ceremony was conducted in Vorkuta by Józef Kuczyński, a priest who had also been released from the camps. In 1956 they returned to Poland.

After most of the Vorkuta camps were closed down, the authorities encouraged free workers to come live above the Arctic Circle, where high salaries and "northern" employment privileges were granted. Mining camps were replaced by mining villages. Most of their inhabitants settled there only temporarily in order to earn some money and then move to more pleasant regions. That is how Vorkuta earned the nickname "*vremenshchik* city," from the Russian word *vremenno*, meaning temporary. After the introduction of a market economy, the laborers' savings began to lose value almost overnight as did hope of buying their own homes in sunny central Russia. Vorkuta turned out to be a trap for those families who had to stay and continued working above the Arctic Circle in Vorkutinskaia, Oktiabrskaia, Severnaia, Vorgashorskaia, Komsomolskaia – mines built by prisoners during Stalinist times. Mine No. 29 is now called the Yur-Shor. Beside the road leading to Yur-Shor the camp cemetery is still intact. The graves of those who on August 1, 1953, were not as lucky as Witold Augusewicz were left behind in the tundra forever.

The Vorkuta industrial concentration camp complex was located 160 kilometers above the Arctic Circle. The Vorkuta coal basin had been built by inmates in the early 1930s and by 1956 included about 15 mines, a city with a population of approximately 15,000 and about 50 camps with more than 50,000 inmates.

The camp guards were most often recruited on three-year contracts after basic military service. The regulations authorized them to shoot without warning at any prisoner who had gone outside the designated work zone, moved too close to the camp fence or strayed too far from a column under escort. The accounts of former prisoners often describe prisoners being shot by guards and escorts.

The officer corps, consisting of soldiers
and NKVD agents, resided with their
families near the camp complexes.

One of the Vorkutlag camps, which had about 2,000 prisoners. On the horizon is Mine No.1, the Kapitalnaia, the largest in the Vorkuta basin. The photograph was taken clandestinely from the top of slagheap of Mine No. 9-10 by the Pole Stanislaw Kialka with a camera that he had built himself.

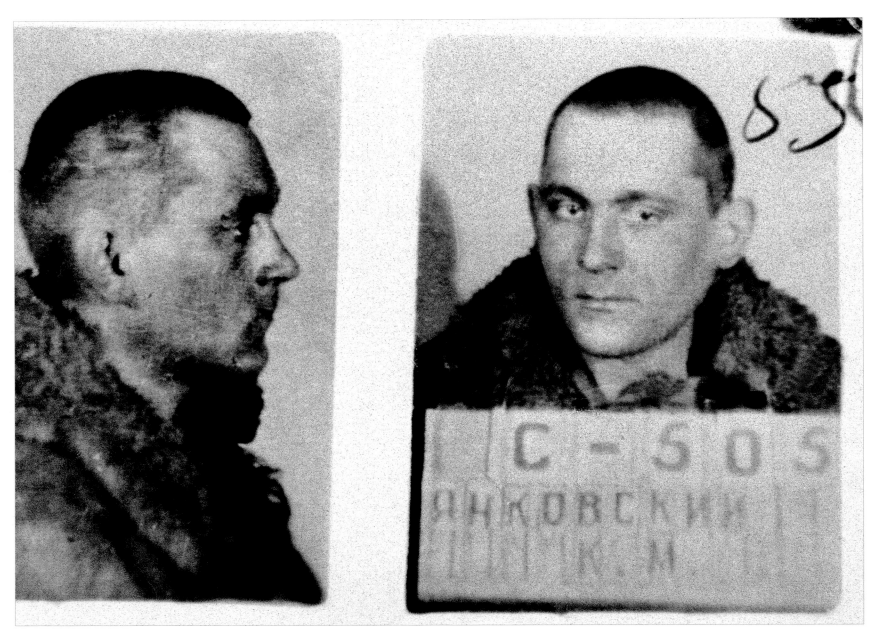

Kazimierz Jankowski, a soldier with the Home
Army's Carpathian Partisan Division. He was
arrested by the NKVD in 1945 in Lwów, sentenced
to 20 years of hard labor in the Vorkutlag. He
returned to Poland in 1956.

Stefan Józefowicz, a Home Army
soldier, was arrested by the NKVD in
1945 and sentenced to death. His
sentence was commuted to 20 years of
hard labor. A prisoner at the Vorkuta
camps, he took part in the strike in the
camp at Mine No. 29 in 1953. He
returned to Poland in 1956.

Prisoners released from the camps.
On the right is Home Army soldier
Wladyslaw Borysiewicz. The other
man is unidentified.

Stanislaw Kialka (left) and Wiktor Han holding arctic
partridges. Photograph taken after their release
from the camp, fall 1956.

Stanislaw Kialka was a soldier of the Polish Home Army.
He was a close collaborator of Alexander Krzyzanowski,
commander of the Home Army's Vilnius District, whose
code name was Wolf and who was responsible for helping
the families of Nazi victims. Kialka was awarded the Silver
Cross "Virtuti Militari," the Silver Cross of Merit with
Swords and the Gallantry Cross. He was arrested by the
Gestapo, then rescued by a group of soldiers from the
Vilnius District. He was wounded during the battle of
Vilnius in July 1944. Then he was arrested by the NKVD
in 1945 and condemned to fifteen years of hard labor in
the camps. In the Vorkultag camps he organized prisoners
to help one another. When he was released in 1955, he
met Wanda Cejko, a liaison officer and nurse of the Home
Army. They married in Poland in 1958. He died in 1980.

After their release from the camps, Polish prisoners were not allowed to leave Vorkuta. They were allowed to move freely within a seven-kilometer radius of their place of residence. They continued working in the mines but they now were paid for their work. The authorities did not begin authorizing their return to Poland until several months after their release.

The cemetery for prisoners and exiles. In the
background is Mine No. 9-10, and on the horizon
is Mine No. 1, the Kapitalnaia.
Dead prisoners were buried in the tundra, and at
their burial a plain post was driven into the ground
with their camp number on it. In 1956 prisoners
released from the camps found the graves of their
comrades and erected crosses.

The graves of Jeremi Odyński and Jan Preuzner, Poles shot while trying to escape from the camp in 1954.

Funeral of an unidentified prisoner who died after his release from the camp. First on the left is Józef Jodko; the rest are unidentified.

Stanislaw Kialka after his release. In the background is the camp and Mine No. 9-10.

Home Army soldiers Jadwiga Olechnowicz
and Witold Augusewicz after their release
from the camps. In the background is the
cemetery for victims of the 1953 camp
strike at Mine No. 29, which was violently
suppressed by the authorities.

Home Army soldiers Natalia
Odyńska and Olgierd Zarzycki
after their release from the
camps. Natalia Odyńska's
brother was shot dead while
trying to escape from the camp.
The couple were married at
Vorkuta in 1956.

Jadwiga Olechnowicz and Edward Muszynski after their release from the camp.

Polish prisoners released from the camps; names unknown.

Released prisoners bought
cameras in the stores of
Vorkuta and took
commemorative photographs.

A group of Poles after their
release from the camps. In
the background are the camp
and mines. From left to right:
Bronislawa Kutiuk, Wanda
Cejko, Franciszek Sitnik,
Barbara Dudycz, Stanislaw
Kialka, Olgierd Zarzycki,
Hanna Szyszko.

A group of Poles, former Vorkuta camp prisoners, shortly before
their return to Poland. From left to right: Witold Augusewicz,
Jadwiga Olechnowicz, Natalia Odyńska, Wanda Cejko, Janina Zuba,
Stanislaw Kuzma, Michal Tatarzycki.

Józef Zwinogrodzki, Home Army soldier, medical doctor, prisoner at
the Vorkuta camps from 1945 to 1956. In the camps he worked as
a doctor. After his return to Poland, he worked for many years at a
surgical clinic in Warsaw.

Henryk Jasiński, a radio
operator for the Home
Army's Vilnius District,
and a prisoner in the
Vorkuta camps from 1945
to 1956. In Red Square,
Moscow, on his way back
to Poland in 1956.

VORKUTA
Historical note

The camps at Vorkuta were established in 1931 to mine mineral coal deposits at the foot of the Arctic Ural Mountains, 160 kilometers above the Arctic Circle in an arctic tundra zone. In the winter the temperatures fall to minus 60 degrees Celsius, the icy winds blow, and for three months a year there is perpetual darkness.

Here, for 25 years prisoners and exiles built from scratch one of the largest coal mining areas in the Soviet Union, including more than 20 mines, the city of Vorkuta, mining villages, power stations, roads and railroads. The Vorkuta complex of camps and mines was part of the vast industrial camp system in the Komi Republic. Alongside Kolyma and Norilsk, Vorkuta was the place where "the most dangerous political criminals" were sent.

For the first 10 years mining in the Vorkuta coal basin was totally ineffective and brought losses, mainly because of transportation difficulties and poorly organized work.

Coal from Vorkuta was carried by narrow-gauge railroad to the port at Vorkuta-Vom on the Usa River. The railroad was in poor condition, and the train took 8-10 hours to travel 64 kilometers. In the summer the coal was loaded onto small barges, the only type of vessel that could negotiate the upper Usa River. Then at the village of Adzva-Vom the coal was unloaded onto the shore and reloaded onto bigger barges that carried it to the mouth of the Usa. There it was again reloaded onto large river barges that took it to the mouth of the Pechora River on the Barents Sea. Then it was loaded onto seagoing ships that took it to Arkhangelsk, from where it was transported into the interior of the USSR by railroad. On its journey from Vorkuta to Arkhangelsk, some 2,300 kilometers, the coal was transferred no fewer than six times. At every stage the inmates manually loaded and unloaded the cargo. Along the same route, but in the opposite direction, supplies, building materials and prisoners were brought to Vorkuta. Because the upper Usa River is only navigable for 40-50 days a year, that was the length of the transportation and supply season for the coal basin. Almost every year a significant amount of the goods failed to reach Vorkuta, which caused work stoppages and food shortages. Only in 1936 did the Soviet government make a decision to build a railroad to Vorkuta, which was completed in 1941.

The prisoners at the Vorkuta region camps did the following work:
• built and operated the Vorkutstroi combine (later known as Vorkutaugol)
• built mines and mined mineral coal
• built the city of Vorkuta, mining villages and an airport
• built two thermal power stations
• built and repaired the railroad connecting Vorkuta and Khalmer Yu
• built power lines
• worked at the sawmill, cement plants, brickyards, repair and woodwork shop
• drilled and loaded/unloaded
• worked at eight state farms
• built barges
• prospected
• designed work in construction offices.

In the second half of the 1950s most of the camps were closed down, but Vorkutlag still existed in 1960. The date of its final closure is not known, because documents relating to the period after January 25, 1960 have not yet been made public.

Published data on the mortality rate among prisoners at the Vorkuta camps are incomplete. In 1942, 1,315 people (5% of the total) died in Vorkutlag; in 1943, 3,948 (15.5%) died; and in 1944, 3,144 (10.5%). Over the next few years the annual average mortality rate was 2-3% of all prisoners. The total number of victims in the Vorkuta camps has not been established.

Chronology

1929

July 6: the steamship *Gleb Boky* departs from the port of Kem on the White Sea with the OGPU's Ukhta Expedition on board. The aim of the expedition is to prospect for oil and other raw materials in the Ukhta River region of the Komi Republic. The expedition members include its leader Sidorov, several managers, guards and 139 prisoners, among them many geologists, mining engineers and topographers. The expedition route is from Kem to Arkhangelsk on the steamship *Gleb Boky*, then from Arkhangelsk to the mouth of the Pechora River on the Barents Sea on the *Umba*, up the Pechora to the mouth of the Izhma River on barges pulled by tugboats, and finally up the Izhma on 18 barges pulled by prisoners walking along the riverbank.

August 21: the expedition reaches its goal, the village of Chibiu (now the city of Ukhta). The expedition base is built. Geological prospecting starts, as well as oil extraction: the work day is 12 hours long, with no days off, and insufficient food supplies. There is a high mortality rate among the prisoners because of hunger, vitamin deficiency and illness.

November 2: prisoner Yakov Yossem-Moroz is appointed head of the OGPU's Ukhta Expedition; he is a Cheka-OGPU officer sentenced to seven years' incarceration for "abuse of power" and "unlawful executions."

1930

There are no data on the number of prisoners accompanying the OGPU's Ukhta Expedition.

Geologist G. A. Chernov discovers rich deposits of mineral coal on the Vorkuta River in the so-called Pechora Basin.

1931

On January 1, the number of prisoners is 824, and on June 1, 982.

March 27: the USSR Labor and Defense Council issues a decree "On the Development of the Coal Mining Industry and the Expansion of Geological Prospecting in the Pechora Basin."

May: an expedition sent from Chibiu led by geologist and prisoner Nikolai Inkin arrives in the Vorkuta River region, to examine the recently discovered coal deposits.

June 6: the Ukhta Expedition is renamed the Ukhta-Pechora Corrective Labor Camp or Ukhtpechlag.

Yakov Yossem-Moroz is appointed head of Ukhtpechlag; his sentence is rescinded and he is reinstated as a member of the All-Union Communist Party (Bolshevik).

1932

In December the number of prisoners at Ukhtpechlag is 13,400, including an unknown number working at Vorkuta.

November 16: a decree of the USSR Labor and Defence Council establishes the OGPU Ukhta-Pechora Company, which is assigned the task of prospecting for and mining natural resources, as well as doing auxiliary work: building roads, railroads, settlements and camps.

Construction of the first primitive mineshaft, "Vorkutinsky rudnik" (Vorkutinsky mine), on the right bank of the Vorkuta River. Geological prospecting for coal deposits at Vorkuta.

1933

On January 1, the number of prisoners at Ukhtpechlag is 23,840, including an unknown number working at Vorkuta.

September 1: industrial mining at the Vorkutinsky Mine gets underway.

The UkhtPechora Corrective Labor Camp Ukhtpechlag is instructed to build the southern section of the railroad from Vorkuta to Yugorsky Shar (the northern section was to be built by OGPU's Vaigach Expedition, but the project was never completed.

The narrow-gauge railroad from the mine to Vorkuta-Vom is completed.
Geological prospecting for coal deposits continues at Vorkuta.

1935

On January 1, the number of prisoners at Ukhtpechlag is 20,730, including an unknown number working at Vorkuta.

Vasily Barabanov is appointed head of the Vorkutinsky Mine (in 1947-1950 he would run the construction of the railroad from Chum to Igarka, the so-called "Road of Death).

1936

On January 1, the number of prisoners at Ukhtpechlag is 21,750, including an unknown number working at Vorkuta.

Building starts for Mine No. 1, the Kapitalnaia, Vorkuta's main mine with a planned annual output of 750,000 tons of coal.

Trotskyite communists, Social Revolutionaries and Mensheviks hold a hunger strike, refuse to go to work and demand that they be given political prisoner status.

1937

On January 1, the number of prisoners at Ukhtpechlag is 31,035, including an unknown number working at Vorkuta.

A special NKVD Troika led by Kashketin issues mass death sentences for prisoners and free workers.

The Trotskyites, Social Revolutionaries and Mensheviks who protested the year before are shot.

1938

On January 1, the number of prisoners at Ukhtpechlag is 54,792, including 15,009 working at Vorkuta as of July 1.

In addition there are 25,199 at Sevzheldorlag (building the railroad to Vorkuta).

The Vorkuta region has a total of 40,208 prisoners.

Yakov Yossem-Moroz, the head of Vorkutlag, is sentenced to death and shot.

Captain of State Security L. A. Tarakhanov is appointed in his place.

Further mass executions take place as part of the Great Purge.

May 10: on the basis of Ukhtpechlag camp units, the Vorkuta-Pechora camp, Vorkutlag, (for coal mining) and the Northern Railroad, Sevzheldorlag, (for building the railroad to Vorkuta) are established.

The multi-branch company Vorkutstroy is established to build and mine the Vorkuta coal basin. L. A. Tarakhanov is appointed head of Vorkutlag and Vorkutstroy.

1939

On January 1, the number of prisoners at Vorkutlag is 17,923, and at Sevzheldorlag 29,405.

The Vorkuta region has a total of 47,328 prisoners.

1940

On January 1, the number of prisoners at Vorkutlag is 16,509, and at Sevzheldorlag 26,310.

In total the Vorkuta region has a total of 42,819 prisoners.

There is an influx of people arrested in the eastern territory of Poland annexed by the USSR in the first phase of the war.

May 14: a separate camp, the North Pechora, or Sevpechlag, is divided off from the Northern Railroad Sevzheldorlag camp, with the task of building the 457-kilometer section of the railroad line from Kozhva to Vorkuta (later inmates at this camp built the railroad lines and sidings in Vorkuta and the surrounding area, including the line to Khalmer-Yu).

1941

On January 1, the number of prisoners at Vorkutlag is 19,080, and at Sevpechlag 34,959.

The Vorkuta region has a total of 54,039 prisoners.

New mines are built and coal mining intensifies because German troops have captured the Donbas Coal Basin in Ukraine. (During the war Vorkutstroi would supply coal for the Baltic and Northern fleets, Leningrad, the north-western and some of the central regions of the USSR.)

Food rations are lowered and there is a high mortality rate among prisoners (which would be maintained until the end of the war).

Construction of Mines No. 2, 3 and 4 begins.

August 12: the USSR Supreme Soviet decrees an amnesty for Polish citizens. Most Polish prisoners are released from the camps, which reinforces the ranks of the Polish Army in the USSR, established under the command of General Wladyslaw Anders.

November 17: the Inta camp, Intalag, is formed by regrouping Vorkutlag camp units responsible for prospecting for and mining coal deposits near Inta.

December 23: The Pechora Mainline Railroad linking Vorkuta with Leningrad and the USSR rail network is completed (in the years that follow it will be constantly improved and upgraded).

1942

On January 1, the number of prisoners at Vorkutlag is 28,588, and at Sevpechlag 102,354, but there are no data on numbers at Intalag.

The Vorkuta region (minus Intalag) has a total of 130,942 prisoners.

Construction of Mines No. 5 and 6 begins.

Power Station TES-1 goes into operation.

1943

On January 1, the number of prisoners at Vorkutlag is 27,793, at Sevpechlag 58,825, and at Intalag 6,502.

The Vorkuta region has a total of 93,120 prisoners.

The number of free workers in the Vorkuta region is about 2,300.

Major General M. M. Maltsev is appointed head of Vorkutlag and Vorkutstroy.

April 19: a decree of the USSR Supreme Soviet introduces the penalty of hard labor regimes (an extended period of hard physical labor and more severe camp regulations) for "supporters of the fascist occupiers"; almost all members of national independence movements in Ukraine and the Baltic republics, Polish Home Army soldiers, as well as Hungarians, Romanians, Czechs and Japanese are sentenced under this decree.

Construction of Mines No. 7, 9, 10 and 12 begins.

November: the town of Vorkuta is granted a municipal charter.

1944

On January 1, the number of prisoners at Vorkutlag is 25,333, at Sevpechlag 23,019, and at Intalag 7,536.

The Vorkuta region has a total of 55,888 prisoners.

March 1: the Vorkutstroi combine is renamed Vorkutaugol.

1945

On January 1: the number of prisoners at Vorkutlag is 39,711, at Sevpechlag 33,598, and at Intalag 9,268.

The Vorkuta region has a total of 82,577 prisoners.

There is a mass influx of prisoners from countries newly taken over by the Red Army: Estonia, Lithuania, Latvia and Poland, and also Germans and Ukrainians.

Construction of Mines No. 17, 18, 19, 25, 26 and 27 begins.

1946

On January 1, the number of prisoners at Vorkutlag is 52,195, at Sevpechlag 34,826, and at Intalag 14,885.

The Vorkuta region has a total of 101,906 prisoners.

A passenger airport is opened at Vorkuta with an air connection to Moscow.

1947

On January 1, the number of prisoners at Vorkutlag is 63,519, at Sevpechlag 56,615, and at Intalag 20,585.

The Vorkuta region has a total of 140,719 prisoners.

Colonel A. D. Kukhtikov is appointed head of Vorkutlag and the Vorkutaugol combine.

1948

On January 1, the number of prisoners at Vorkutlag is 62,525, at Sevpechlag 47,815, and at Intalag 18,656. The Vorkuta region has a total of 128,966 prisoners.

February 28: The Inta Corrective Labor Camp, *Intalag*, is changed to Special Camp No. 1, the so-called "Mineral Camp," or Minlag, by order of the USSR Ministry of Foreign Affairs establishing Special Camps for political prisoners (where a more stringent regime was enforced similar to that of a prison. The prisoners wore camp numbers sewn on their clothes in three places – hat, knee and back – and were used for especially hard labor).

August 27: by order of the USSR Ministry of Foreign Affairs, dated February 27, Special Camp No. 6, the River Camp, or Rechlag, is established on the basis of some of the Vorkutlag camps.

1949

On January 1, the number of prisoners at Vorkutlag is 66,330, at Rechlag 7,474, at Sevpechlag 39,436, and at Minlag 24,112.

The Vorkuta region has a total of 137,352 prisoners.

Mines No. 12, 14, 16 and 29 are built.

1950

On January 1, the number of prisoners at Vorkutlag is 62,676, at Rechlag 25,024, at Sevpechlag 42,028, and at Minlag 28,371.

The Vorkuta region has a total of 158,099 prisoners.

July 24: the Pechora Corrective Labor Camp, or Pechorlag, is established by combining the Northern Railroad Camp Sevzheldorlag and the North Pechora Corrective Labor Camp Sevpechlag.

Mines No. 30 and 32 are built.

1951

On January 1, the number of prisoners at Vorkutlag is 72,940, at Rechlag 27,547, at Pechorlag 59,408, and at Minlag 33,056.

The Vorkuta region has a total of 192,951 prisoners.

1952

On January 1, the number of prisoners at Vorkutlag is 41,677; at Rechlag,

35,459; at Pechorlag 38,926; and at Minlag 34,448.

The Vorkuta region has a total of 150,510 prisoners.

Colonel S.I. Degtiev is appointed head of Vorkutlag and the Vorkutaugol combine.

1953

On January 1, the number of prisoners at Vorkutlag is 36,861; at Rechlag 35,451; at Pechorlag 47,001; and at Minlag 31,834.

The Vorkuta region has a total of 151,147 prisoners.

Lieutenant-Colonel G. M. Prokopiev is appointed head of Vorkutlag and the Vorkutaugol combine.

March 5: death of Stalin.

March 27: a decree is issued by the USSR Supreme Soviet on an amnesty that in practice does not include political prisoners. A large number of criminal prisoners are released from the camps. There is a distinct improvement in conditions within the camps.

April 1, 1953: the Vorkutaugol combine is disconnected from the management of the USSR Ministry of Foreign Affairs and overseen by the Ministry of the Coal Industry.

July: prisoners at seven of the seventeen camp groups within Vorkutlag go on strike (in the camps at Mines No. 4, 7, 12, 14, 16 and 29 and the TES-2 Power Station, for a total of 15,600 prisoners). The strikers demand a review and reduction of sentences for political prisoners, and as a result their release from the camps.

August 1: the strike at Mine No. 29 is violently suppressed: troops open machine-gun fire on a crowd of prisoners, and at least 66 people are killed, with 134 wounded. The strikes at other camps are suppressed by threats, persuasion and the introduction of minor concessions.

1954

On January 1, the number of prisoners at Vorkutlag is 33,087, at Rechlag 37,654, at Pechorlag 23,678, and at Minlag 28,055.

In total in the Vorkuta region there are 122,474 prisoners.

May 26: Special Camp No. 6, the so-called River Camp, Rechlag, is closed.

1955

On January 1, the number of prisoners at *Vorkutlag* is 52,453, at *Pechorlag* 18,505, and at *Minlag* 15,259.

The Vorkuta region has a total of 86,217 prisoners.

The USSR government issues a decree allowing most of the Poles in the USSR, including those imprisoned in the camps, to leave for Poland.

1956

On January 1, the number of prisoners at Vorkutlag is 50,515, at Pechorlag 10,046, and at Minlag 10,327.

The Vorkuta region has a total of 70,888 prisoners.

Sentences are gradually reviewed and Polish prisoners are released.

1957

On January 1, the number of prisoners at Vorkutlag is 49,646, at Pechorlag 7,389, and at Minlag 6,819.

The Vorkuta region has a total of 63,854 prisoners.

March 6: Special Camp No. 1, the so-called Mineral Camp, Minlag, is closed.

March 27: a treaty is signed by the USSR and Polish governments concerning the timetable and means for further repatriation of Polish nationals from the USSR.

1958

There are no data on the number of prisoners at Vorkutlag or at Pechorlag.

1959

On January 1, the number of prisoners at Vorkutlag is 20,785 and at Pechorlag 12,773. The Vorkuta region has a total of 33,558 prisoners.

Colonel P. Y. Titov is appointed head of Vorkutlag and the Vorkutaugol combine.

The Pechora camp Pechorlag is closed.

1960

On 1 January the number of prisoners at Vorkutlag is 15,338.

Sources :

1. Sergey Filipov and Sergei Sigachov, *Vorkutsky* ITL ["The Vorkuta Corrective Labor Camp"], Sergei Krivenko *Ukhtyskaya Ekspeditsiya OGPU* ["OGPU's Ukhta Expedition"], Dimitri Shkapov, Rechny Lager ["The River Camp"] in *Lagry.* ["The Prison Camps. An Encyclopedic Guide"], issued by the "Memorial" Center for Research, Information and Dissemination (NIPC) in Moscow, jointly edited by Nikita Okhotin and Arseny Roginsky.

2. A. Kaneva, Ukhtpechlag 1929-1938 in the historical almanac *Zvenia*, Moscow 1991.

3. Siergiej Sigaczow, Lagry OGPU-NKWD-MWD ZSRR w regionie workuckim ["OGPU-NKVD-USSR Ministry of Internal Affairs prison camps in the Vorkuta region"] in *Wiezniowie lagrów w rejonie Workuty* ["Prisoners at camps in the Vorkuta region"] edited by Agnieszka Knyt (Osrodek KARTA) and Aleksander Gurianow (NIPC Memorial), in cooperation with Jewgienija Chajdarowa, Memorial Vorkuta), Anna Dzienkiewicz and Anna Piekarska, published by Osrodek Karta, Warsaw 1999.

4. Pavel Negretov, Pochtovy Yashchik Nr 223. Kak nachinalas Vorkuta ["PO Box 223. How Vorkuta began"], in *Pechalnaia Pristan* ["Melancholy Harbor"], edited by I.L. Kuznetsov, Komi knizhnoe izdatelstvo, Syktyvkar 1991.

We worked in the forge. We were dying of hunger. One of the prisoners caught a rat, roasted it on the fire and ate it, entrails and all. On our way back to camp he broke away from the column of prisoners and went off into the tundra. This was a means of suicide used by the prisoners. Naturally, the escorts shot him.

Bernard Grzywacz, prisoner at Vorkutlag from 1945 to 1957.

Sometimes a musician played the accordion at the gate as the prisoners were on their way out to work. One day we were waiting in a column, and nearby stood a horse harnessed to a sled covered with canvas. Suddenly the musician extended the accordion to its full width, making a loud noise. Startled, the horse jerked the sled and frozen corpses tumbled out like logs from under the tarpaulin. The whole column of prisoners waiting at the gate began to laugh hysterically.

Wanda Kialka, prisoner at Vorkutlag from 1945 to 1956.

In the first year I realized that anyone with a West European upbringing, mindset and attitude to life could not survive more than two or three years in the camp. I realized that I must revert by centuries, to the time when the principle of an eye for an eye and the survival of the fittest determined who lives. This enabled me to survive for five and a half years, while hundreds of others perished.

October 11, 1950

I think about our meeting a lot, and about the changes time has inflicted on us. All the things I once regarded as the ideals and principles of life have been reduced to dust. What have I filled the void with? What is the meaning of life now?

November 16, 1953

Endless cold and rain. I dream about pine forests.

July 7, 1954

Yesterday at 8 o'clock we were taken out (24 of us) beyond the camp zone.

September 1954

From the letters of Wladyslaw Haydenberg to his wife. The author was able to correspond with his wife because she lived in the USSR. Sending letters to Poland was impossible. Stefania and Wladyslaw Haydenberg returned to Poland in 1955.

Yesterday I appeared before the committee and I was freed. It's hard to describe what it feels like, especially just after being let out. I felt a sort of blind, dumb joy, and at the same time some insecurity, but I am actually at liberty and no one's following me; I can come and go as I like. Everything seems fine, but I don't feel the sort of joy I had imagined. I'd like to leave as soon as possible.

From the diary of Boleslaw Koltun

My first trees! Yellow leaves... For 11 years I hadn't seen normal trees, only as props in the mine, stripped of leaves or needles, with no branches. The feeling was incredible.

From an account by Olgierd Zarzycki

I took a good look at the Polish-Soviet border. I was thinking of the hundreds of crazy people in the camps who used to dream of escaping, or even tried to. If I were to show them that border now, they'd realize it would have been easier to reach the Moon.
*   I fear this new, unfamiliar life that I've longed for with all my heart and soul. I know I'll feel isolated and different, and that all sorts of things that mean nothing to those who are free will be big problems for me. I feel a sort of regret – could it be for the past few years?*

From the memoirs of Henryk Urbanowicz

Sources: Based on: Tomasz Gleb and Malgorzata Strasz, Powrót ze Wschodu. Inaczej ni ż w snach ["Returning from the East. Different from in our dreams"], in historical quarterly *Karta*, No. 10, 1993.

VORKUTA
memories

Vorkuta

A camp watchtower.

The remains of a camp in the tundra.

The cemetery near Mine No. 29, now the Yur-Shor Mine (on the horizon), where prisoners shot during the suppression of the strike in 1953 are buried. Posts were driven into the prisoners' graves with their camp numbers inscribed on them, but with no names.

The house at No. 5 Kirov Street in Vorkuta. In the 1950s this was the site of the camp cemetery near Mine No. 40, where Jeremi Odyński and Jan Preuzner were buried, shot trying to escape from the camp in 1954.

A cross erected at a prisoner's burial site by the family or by camp comrades.

Women sorting coal at the Yur-Shor Mine; in Stalinist times it was Mine No. 29.

Miners at the Yur-Shor Mine.

Yuri Voroshilov, Communist Party
member, mayor of Vorkuta.

Vitaly Troshin, chief architect
of Vorkuta, initiator of the
construction of monuments
to the victims of Vorkutlag,
president of the Vorkuta branch
of the Memorial Society that
helps victims of political
repression and protects
human rights in Russia.

The Stroitelny mining village
near the Severnaya Mine
(on the horizon), which in
Stalinist times was Mine
No. 5.

423

Miners' monument in Vorkuta's central square.

Anna Krikun, a Ukrainian
imprisoned in Vorkutlag from
1943 to 1956, camp number
JU-683. In the background is
the old Brickyard No. 2, where
she worked as a prisoner at
the women's hard labor camp.
After her release from the
camp she stayed in Vorkuta
and worked at Mine No. 17.
Now retired, she is a board
member of the Memorial
Society's Vorkuta branch.

Vladimir Timonin and his daughter, in front of the boiler room at Mine No. 17, where he worked for nine years as prisoner number 2Z-883. In 1943-1945 Vladimir Timonin was a prisoner in the Nazi concentration camp at Stutthof, and after returning to the Soviet Union he was arrested as a "traitor to the fatherland" and sentenced to 15 years in the camps. From 1945 to 1955 he was imprisoned at Vorkutlag. After his release he settled in Vorkuta, worked in the coal basin administration and achieved the position of deputy director of the Vorkutaugol Coal Company. Now retired, he is vice-president of the Memorial Society's Vorkuta branch.

Pavel Negretov, a prisoner at Vorkutlag from 1946 to 1955, camp number JU-491. In the background is Mine No. 40, now the Vorkutinskaya mine, where Pavel Negretov worked for nine years as a prisoner, and for the next 16 years as a free worker in the geology department. After his release from the camp he settled in Vorkuta, and then received a correspondence degree in history from Leningrad University. He wrote the first independent academic paper on the history of Vorkutlag, published in samizdat in 1975, and then reprinted in Great Britain. He also wrote a collection of camp memoirs entitled *All Roads Lead to Vorkuta*, published in the West. These publications resulted in his being harassed by the KGB well into the 1980s.

Leonid Kossovsky, a Ukrainian
born in 1947 in the
Predshakhtnaya camp at Vorkuta
(seen in the background). After
he was born, he was sent to an
orphanage. His grandmother
later retrieved him to bring him
up. His mother was a prisoner
at the Vorkutlag camps from
1944 to 1955. His father is
unknown. After her release from
the camp, his mother settled in
Vorkuta. Leonid Kossovsky
returned to Vorkuta at the age
of 17. He works as a mining
equipment mechanic.

Dimitri Usenko, a Ukrainian, a prisoner at Vorkutlag from 1945 to 1955, camp number C-286. In the background is a bust of Lenin standing in front of the entrance to Mine No. 11, now called the Yuzhnaia mine, where Dimitri Usenko worked as a prisoner for 10 years. After his release he graduated from the Leningrad Institute of Metallurgy and returned to Vorkuta. He worked in management at the mines and was awarded several Soviet Orders of Labor. His family was active in the Ukrainian national independence movement. His mother spent 10 years in the Vorkuta camps; his father died of starvation in a camp in the Urals; and his pregnant sister was tortured to death during interrogation by the NKVD.

Wanda Kialka, born Cejko, at the grave of
her husband, Stanislaw Kialka, in Wroclaw.

Józef Zwinogrodzki (right) at his
apartment in Warsaw with Henryk
Jasiński.

Jadwiga and Witold
Augusewicz at their
apartment in Slupsk.

Natalia Zarzycka, born
Odyńska, in front of
the apartment block
where she lives in
Warsaw. Her husband
Olgierd Zarzycki
organized the first
meetings of former
Gulag prisoners in
Poland in the 1980s.
He died in 1990.

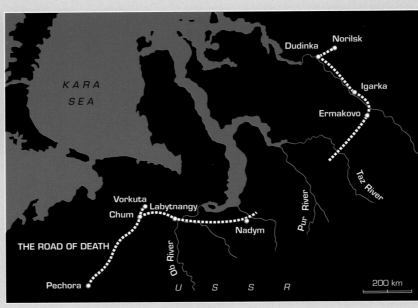

KARA
SEA

Norilsk
Dudinka
Igarka
Ermakovo
Taz River
Pur River
Vorkuta
Labytnangy
Chum
Nadym
Ob River
THE ROAD OF DEATH
Pechora
U S S R
200 km

THE ROAD OF DEATH

THE ROAD OF DEATH
1947-1953

Rusty locomotives forsaken in virgin forest in the wilderness. A railway line is sinking into the marshes, its bridges collapsed, its rails bent, and trees growing on the tracks. Dozens of deserted prison camps, greenery forcing its way into the chinks of the ruins, empty barracks, discarded prison hats, gloves and bowls. Hundreds of kilometers of railroad tracks leading nowhere. That is how the ultimate Stalinist *stroika*, or construction project looks today; it is the Great Northern Railroad, later called "The Road of Death." The history of this construction project is a testimony of the cruelty and absurdity of Soviet totalitarianism.

After the Second World War, Stalin decided to build a large seaport on the arctic shore of Siberia, a location chosen primarily for strategic reasons. His finger came to rest on the mouth of the Ob River, where it empties into the Arctic Ocean. A few months later a contingent of several hundred prisoners arrived by sea and found themselves in the tundra of the Yamal Peninsula, on the coast of the Golf of Ob. Throughout the summer, they unloaded tons of building materials, which had arrived from Murmansk and Arkhangelsk via the Northern Seaway. Because there was no pier, men stood waist high in water, hoisting crates from barges to shore. In the fall it became apparent that the Golf of Ob was too shallow for seagoing ships. Waters in the coastal zone ran no more than five meters deep, falling as low as half a meter in unfavorable winds. This had not been properly checked in advance. The plan to construct a port on the Golf of Ob was called off. The prisoners spent the arctic winter in tents and dugouts in the tundra.

Then, Stalin chose a place called Igarka, 1,300 kilometers to the east, on the mouth of the Enisei River as the site for his arctic port. First, over three years, a railroad connecting Salekhard and Igarka was to be built, and then, the seaport itself. Shipyards for repairs would follow.

This project was assigned to a specialize unit in the Gulag: the Chief Administration of Railroad Construction Camps, run by Naftaly Frenkel, former head of construction at the White Sea Canal, the Volga-Don Canal, as well as other projects. Frenkel, who had miraculously survived the Great Purge, while all his Cheka colleagues were shot, knew that should the project fail Stalin could condemn the entire unit to death. Arseny Barabanov and Vasily Samodurov, who were directly in charge of construction, also knew this. The Road of Death, like every great *stroika*, was a race against time and a fight for life: both for the lives of the prisoners working at a murderous pace, and for the bosses, terrified of being tried and executed for sabotage.

436

This time the project was not only gigantic, but also full of unique technical difficulties. The railroad would have to run across the wild Siberian wasteland to the latitude of the Arctic Circle. The entire route from Salekhard on the Ob to Igarka on the Yenisei had a grand total of four fishing and hunting villages, with only a few houses in each. There weren't even any maps of the region. Aerial photographs taken at the last minute at the request of the architects were used instead. The *stroika* was launched with inexplicable haste, without either plan, or regard for cost, or technical design. Plans were drawn on the fly as construction proceeded; they were completed only in 1952, when more than half the railroad had already been built!

Seventy thousand prisoners laid the railway line simultaneously from two directions: from Salekhard in the west and from Igarka in the east. The plan was to join up in the middle of the West Siberian Lowlands on the Pur River. In the summer, prisoners dispatched deep into the marshy taiga carried food on their backs and slept in huts; mud filled their boots, their clothing never dried out, and the mosquitoes and Siberian gnats never gave them a moment's peace. First of all they built a telephone line between Igarka and Salekhard, and then over 100 camps every few kilometers along the entire route. But since their work was only provisionally mapped out, they knew in advance it would have to be redone. In a total wasteland on the Taz River, the prisoners built a pier and unloaded locomotives and train cars, arriving by barge, which were never to leave that spot. There they would remain forever, on a blind section of track in the Siberian wilderness.

The arctic climate made the situation even worse. In the winter months the mercury in the thermometer fell to minus 50 degrees C and blizzards raged, piling up two to three-meter-high snowdrifts in a few hours. Snow covered the tracks, camps and stores. Transporting building materials and provisions to such distant, inaccessible places caused enormous difficulties. In the summer the snow-covered Siberian wastes changed into impassable flood plains and swamps. In the winter trains were run across ice routes over the Ob near Salekhard. A wooden construction was set up on the thick ice over the frozen river, and then doused with water so that it turned into a sort of ice bridge, on which tracks were laid and trains were set in motion. In the early spring, before the ice on the river began to shift, the crossing would be dismantled.

Construction of the Great Northern Railroad progressed with great difficulty. In the spring, huge amounts of melting snow would cause floods that washed away the railroad and destroyed the bridges. In the summer the permafrost would melt under the embankment, which would then start to shift, and the tracks would buckle. The trains could only move at speeds of up to 15 kilometers an hour, and even then they would come off the rails. Every year, as tens of hundreds of kilometers of track were laid, more and more labor and resources had to be allocated for endless repairs on sections that had already gone into service. The great *stroika* floundered in the Siberian snow and mud.

Despite this disastrous state of affairs, dispatches to Moscow would report the completion of the sections of the Great Northern Railroad. Ceremonies were held to announce the opening of new stations and bridges; locomotives would make triumphant entrances decorated with portraits of Stalin. There were speeches, ovations and awards. Brass bands would play. Engineers and officials, even those in Moscow, must have realized that these charades concealed an abortive and unprofitable enterprise. But no one had the courage to tell Stalin. The absurd farce of the Road of Death came to an end with the death of the leader. Two weeks after his funeral the Soviet government suspended the construction project and ordered its immediate closure. Once again, haste wreaked organizational havoc, incurring further losses. Locomotives, trains, vast amounts of building material, fuel and provisions that could not be moved were left behind in the taiga. Along the route of the Road of Death villages, engine sheds, railroad stations, over 100 camps and the town of Ermakovo on the Enisei were all abandoned – a total of almost 1,500 buildings, most of which were later destroyed.

The Road of Death was financed by the state budget "according to expenditures incurred," i.e., without limit. It became an enormous burden for the Soviet Union's postwar economy. A sub-arctic railroad might have been practical if it had been well planned and well designed, but the lack of preparation and the haste with which it was begun caused the project's inevitable disaster. Even if the line had been finished, there would have been nothing to transport across the wild, uninhabited regions of northern Siberia, except for supplies for the port at Igarka. Had it been extended to the Norilsk Metallurgical Combine, as planned for a later date, revenues from the connection would never have covered construction costs and maintenance expenses.

But the true absurdity of the Road of Death lay elsewhere. The line from Salekhard to Igarka was only the first stage in the Trans-Arctic Railroad, which was to cross the entire length of Siberia at the latitude of the Arctic Circle from the Urals to Chukhotka. This was an enormous project conceived by an aging dictator. Here is how it was justified at the time: *It is hard to overestimate the role of this route in assimilating extensive areas and natural resources in the north. Building the Salekhard-Igarka line will also bring about such great changes in the life of those regions that at present we have no way of foreseeing their dimensions or consequences. In the future, this line will be the main part of the railroad linking the northern coast of the Pacific Ocean and the central and northwestern regions.*

Even if at other construction sites in the USSR, Stalin's orders, his subordinates' fear and thousands of slaves were enough to carry the project through to completion, on the Road of Death this method did not work – Siberian nature put up too much resistance. The construction of the Great Northern Railroad ended in a total fiasco. Today the Road of Death has become a sort of allegory for the history of Soviet communism – a road built contrary to common sense, using slave labor, paid for by millions of victims and leading nowhere.

Officers of the Northern Administration of Railroad Construction Camps. Second from the right is Colonel Vasily Barabanov, head of the Great Northern Railroad construction project. Salekhard, 1947.

Citizens of Salekhard on the Ob River celebrating the opening of the railroad station and the start of the Salekhard-Igarka Railroad project. Salekhard, 1949. Banner on the arch reads: "Glory to the Great Stalin". Banner on the locomotive reads: "Forward to communism."

A group of officers and managers of the eastern section of the project. Ermakovo, 1949.

Start of construction of Ermakovo on the Enisei River, the base for the eastern section of the construction project, 1949.

A group of officers with the construction directors of the eastern section. Ermakovo, 1949.

Unloading barges at Cape Kamenny, 1948.

Supplies for construction of the railroad running across the Siberian wasteland at the latitude of the Arctic Circle were provided in various ways. Above all, goods were transported by river: by boat in the summer and by trucks over the ice in the winter. When that was impossible, caravans of caterpillar tractors were sent. In the summer the prisoner convoys traveled by Trans-Siberian railway to Krasnoiarsk and by barge along the Enisei to Ermakovo, or by ship across the Arctic Ocean. Then they went up the Siberian rivers by barge to rejoin the railroad route. In winter when the Enisei was frozen, supplies for the eastern construction could only be brought in by air. In order to maintain supplies for the western section in the winter, the Ob River was crossed by laying railroad tracks on the ice, reinforced with wooden beams.

Building the city of Ermakovo on the Enisei River. In the first year, housing had to be built for the prisoners and more than 10,000 free workers.

Transporting earth to build
the railroad embankment.

Marking out the route
of the railroad.

Shovels, wheelbarrows and the
prisoners' muscle power were
the basic building resources for
the Road of Death.

The Road of Death was improvised – the tracks were laid on a low, unstrengthened embankment in order to advance as quickly as possible into the depths of the Siberian taiga. This made it possible to guarantee easy transport of materials and supplies to distant places, and also to report to Moscow on the rapid progress of the work. Later the railway line had to be rebuilt.

Building the railway line connecting Chum and Labytnangy, 1947.

Damage caused by the spring thaw.

A spring flood in the Nadym River region in the western section of the Road of Death.
The route of the highway crossed dozens of rivers and streams in the West Siberian
Lowlands. A sawmill in Salekhard produced ready-made wooden bridges, which were
assembled on the spot, even when the railroad embankment was not yet ready.

THE ROAD OF DEATH
Historical note

The Road of Death, or the Great Northern Railroad, built in 1947-1953, was the last of Stalin's great construction projects. The railway line running across the West Siberian Lowlands at the latitude of the Arctic Circle was to connect the station at Chum on the Pechora Railway line, Salekhard on the Ob River and Igarka on the Enisei River, where a seaport was to be built. The Chum-Salekhard-Igarka line was to be the first section of the Trans-Arctic Railroad, running from the Urals to Chukhotka, and intended to be the land equivalent of the Northern Seaway.

In 1947-1949 the section from the station at Chum to the settlement of Labytnangy on the Ob River was completed. Starting from 1949, the railroad was built from two directions simultaneously, from Salekhard and from Igarka, with the aim of linking up in the middle of the route on the River Pur. In 1947-1953 a total of about 900 kilometers of railroad were built. In March 1953 building work was stopped in view of the vast expense, technical problems and pointlessness of the enterprise in economic terms. Today only the short, western section from the station at Seida (formerly Chum) to the village of Labytnangy on the Ob River is in service. It is 190 kilometers long.

The Road of Death construction project ended the 20-year active period of the camp-industrial complexes in the USSR. In the early 1950s, the camp system as a structure in the USSR economy was in crisis. In 1951-1952 not one of the large camp-production administrations subordinate to the MVD (Ministry of Internal Affairs) had managed to complete its plan. After the death of Stalin, the USSR Council of Ministers closed down 15 of the MVD's production administrations and put a halt to many large construction projects that "did not meet the urgent requirements of the economy." In the next few years the camp-production complex underwent further disintegration.

Apart from building the Great Northern Railroad, prisoners did the following work:
- built a second track on the Pechora-Vorkuta section
- built a communications line from Igarka to Salekhard
- laid cables across the Enisei River
- built the town of Ermakovo on the Yenisei, and housing at Igarka and Salekhard
- built a river loading base, a cold store facility and warehouses at Salekhard
- deepened approaches to the harbor in the Labytnangy and Salekhard areas
- built stores and housing at the village of Urengoi
- worked in forestry and wood processing.

The number of prisoners working on the Road of Death totaled about 70,000. Over 50 percent of the workforce were political prisoners; 15 percent were sentenced because of a decree "on protecting socialist property," which made it possible to issue long sentences, even for stealing a small amount of corn at a kolkhoz; and about 35 percent were criminal prisoners. To increase labor productivity a system of deductions was introduced: for each day a work brigade completed 125 percent of the norm, the prisoners had two days deducted from their sentences; and for 150 percent of the norm, they had three days deducted. The number of victims of the Road of Death has not been established.

Chronology

1947

There are no data on the number of prisoners.

February 4: a decree is issued by the USSR Council of Ministers regarding the construction of a large port on the Northern Seaway and a railway line leading to it.

February 17: work by the Northern Project Research Expedition begins, run by the MVD and led by Colonel A. A. Farafontev. The expedition takes aerial photographs and maps out the route of the railroad. The Expedition of the Northern Seaway Chief Administration also starts work, seeking sites for a port on the Golf of Ob.

April 22: a resolution is issued by the USSR Council of Ministers on constructing a port on Cape Kamenny, a 700-kilometer railway line between Chum and Labytnangy, as well as a secondary line connecting Yar Sale, Novy Port and Cape Kamenny.

April 28: the Northern Administration of Railroad Construction Camps is established; it is to build the Chum-Labytnangy line. Colonel Vasily Barabanov is appointed head of the camp.

May 13: railroad construction begins with the station at Chum.

September: the Arctic Corrective Labor Camp Zapolarlag at Cape Kamenny is assigned to construct the port on the Golf of Ob. Captain V. V. Samodurov is appointed head of Zapolarlag.

December 3: the Chum-Labytnangy railway section (190 kilometers) opens for train traffic.

1948

There are no data on the number of prisoners.

Construction of the railroad connecting Yar Sale, Novy Port and Cape Kamenny begins. Prison camps, administration buildings, bridges and railroad stations are built. Building materials, people and equipment are transported by ship from Murmansk and Arkhangelsk to Cape Kamenny. Autumn: the plan to build the port on Cape Kamenny is abandoned because of the shallow water in the Golf of Ob.

October 1: the Arctic Corrective Labor Camp Zapolarlag is closed (the prisoners are not evacuated until the spring).

1949

On January 1, the number of prisoners is 79,053, including 50,019 at Construction Site No. 501 (Ob camp), and 29,034 at Construction Site No. 503 (Enisei camp).

January 29: a decree is issued by the USSR to build a port at Igarka and the Great Northern Railroad connecting Salekhard and Igarka, (about 1,300 kilometers long to continue the Chum-Labytnangy section) and then the section connecting Igarka and the Norilsk Metallurgical Combine. The construction will be financed by the state budget "according to expenditures incurred," i.e., without limits. The deadline planned for the completion of the Salekhard-Igarka lines is the end of 1952. The port and ship repair yards at Igarka are to be built in 1953-1955.

Technical criteria for the Great Northern Railroad: a single-track railroad line with summer ferry and winter ice crossings for the Ob and Yenisei Rivers; sidings for trains to pass each other on average every 12 kilometers; and stations every 40-60 kilometers – in total 28 railroad stations, 106 sidings and 10 engine sheds. The average speed of trains is 40 kilometers per hour, with 12 trains running daily in both directions.

February 5: the Ob Corrective Labor Camp at Construction Site No. 501 with its headquarters in Salekhard, and the Enisei Corrective Labor Camp at Construction Site No. 503 at Igarka are established. Colonel V. V. Samodurov is appointed head of the Ob camp, and Major A. V. Artamonov head of the Enisei camp.

November 12: the Enisei camp is closed, and replaced by Northern Administration of Camps at Construction Site No. 503 with its headquarters in Ermakovo on the Yenisei River. Vasily A. Barabanov is head of the camp.

A large-scale operation is undertaken to transport people, equipment, and materials to the eastern section of the construction site. Prisoners, materials and machinery are transported by the Trans-Siberian Railroad to Krasnoiarsk, then by barges up the Enisei. On the left bank of the river, 65 kilometers south of Igarka, the town of Ermakovo is built, the main base for the eastern section of the construction.

The railroad route is mapped out and a telephone line is constructed between from Salekhard and Igarka.

Prison camps are built every 5-7 kilometers along the entire route from Salekhard to Igarka.

1950

On January 1, the number of prisoners is 70,329, including 41,203 at Construction Site No. 501 (Ob camp) and 29,126 at Construction Site No. 503 (Enisei camp).

Lieutenant-Colonel A. I. Borovitsky is appointed head of the Northern Administration of Corrective Labor Camps Construction Site No. 503.

The construction of Ermakovo is completed, including a brickyard, sawmill and machine shop.

Construction of the Salekhard-Igarka Railroad continues.

1951

On January 1, the number of prisoners is 70,492, including 41,718 at Construction Site No. 501 (Ob camp) and 28,774 at Construction Site No. 503 (Enisei camp).

The telephone line is completed, enabling communications between Igarka, Salekhard and Moscow.

Large bridges are built across the Makovskaia, Sukharikha, Turukhan, Barabanikha and Nadym Rivers, and 20 concrete and several dozen wooden bridges are completed across smaller rivers. The engine shed at Ermakovo is completed.

Four ferries are delivered to Salekhard and Igarka by ship along the Northern Seaway, specially designed to take trains across the Ob and the Enisei.

The "Arctiproject" office, subordinate to the Northern Seaway Administration, completes the design for the seaport at Igarka.

1952

On January 1, the number of prisoners is 27,690, including 13,499 at Construction Site No. 501 (Ob camp) and 14,191 at Construction Site No. 503 (Enisei camp).

January 1: the Chief Camp Administration of Railway Construction (GULZDS), which oversees Construction Sites No. 501 and 503 establishes the total cost of the Salekhard-Igarka railroad at 6,536,600,000 rubles; half of the money has already been spent, and the remainder is required for its completion.

The following sections of the railway line are opened for train traffic: Salekhard-Nadym (350 kilometers), Igarka-Ermakovo (65 kilometers) and Ermakovo-Yanov Stan (160 kilometers).

July 21: all camp units of Construction Site No. 503 are subordinated to the Ob Corrective Labor Camp.

1953

On January 1, the number of prisoners at the Ob Construction Site No. 501 camp is 12,725.

There are no data for the northern Construction Site No. 503 camp.

Lieutenant-Colonel M. V. Samuylov is appointed head of the Ob Corrective Labor Camp, followed by Colonel D. M. Loydin (as of May 19).

March 5: Stalin dies.

March 25: a decree is issued by the USSR Council of Ministers suspending construction of the Salekhard-Igarka Railroad. The deadline for closure of the construction project is September 1.

March 27: a decree on amnesty is issued by the USSR Supreme Soviet; in practice, it does not include political prisoners. A large number of criminal prisoners are released from the camps.

Conditions in the camps improve.

1954

February 12, the Ob Corrective Labor Camp is closed.

1955

A resolution by the USSR Council of Ministers is issued to maintain train traffic on the Chum-Labytnangy line (190 kilometers) and the Igarka-Salekhard telephone line, which is transferred from the MVD to the Ministry of Communications.

1965-1967

Most of the tracks and ties on the eastern section of the Road of Death are dismantled and removed by the Norilsk Metallurgical Combine.

Sources :

1. Dmitry Shkapov, *Obski ITL* ["Ob Corrective Labor Camp"], *Severnoe Upravlenie ITL i stroika 503* ["Northern Administration of Corrective Labor Camps and Construction Site 503"], *Zapolarny ITL i stroika 503* ["Arctic Corrective Labor Camp and Construction Site 503"] in *Lagry* ["The Prison Camps. An Encyclopedic Guide"], issued by the Memorial Center for Research, Information and Dissemination (NIPC) in Moscow, jointly edited by Nikita Okhotin and Arseny Roginsky.

2. A. Berzin, *Doroga v nekuda. Materialy o stroitelstve zheleznoi dorogi Salekhard-Igarka. 1947-1953* ["The Road to Nowhere. Information on the Construction of the Salekhard-Igarka Railroad. 1947-1953"] in the periodical *Voprosy istorii, estestvoznania i tekhniki* ["Issues of History, Natural History and Technology"], special edition, USSR Academy of Sciences, Moscow 1990.

3. *Stroika nr 503. Dokumenty. Materialy. Issledovania* ["Construction Site 503. Documents, Information, Research"], a collection edited by M. Mishechin, published by Grotesk, Krasnoyarsk 2000.

4. Alexandr Vologodsky, *Zheleznaa doroga* ["The Railroad"], unpublished text.

Spring flooding in the Nadym basin on the section of the Road of Death.

Our locomotive is hurtling
Towards Communism Station.
We know of no other way.
With rifles in our hands.

Popular Soviet song

An abandoned locomotive
on the tracks of the Road
of Death.

An abandoned prison camp.

A log road leading through
the marsh to the camp.

A watchtower.

470

Prisoners' graves. At the burial
site the camp administrators
erected a post with a sign giving
only the prisoner's file number.

Prisoners' bowls.

The offices of the Department of Culture and Education, which was responsible for propaganda in the camp: it organized political lectures, celebrations of communist festivals and "socialist work competitions" between prisoner work brigades.

Banner (top) reads: "Love a book – a source of knowledge. Only knowledge saves; it alone can make us strong in spirit, honest and wise."

Banners (lower left) read: "Long live our mighty fatherland, the USSR", "Fulfilling the fifth Five-Year Plan marks a great step forward on the road from socialism to communism," "In the USSR labor is a matter of honor and glory, a matter of courage and heroism." (lower right) "...19th Party Congress."

Prisoners' boots.

Decoration in the prisoners' barracks.

Camp accounting forms on the floor of the
spets-chast, the special department.

Two-story wooden bunks
in the prisoners' barracks.

An isolation cell.

The barracks were 40 meters long
and divided into two sections with
separate entrances. Each section
included two rows of two-story
wooden bunks for 80 prisoners
and a brick-built stove.

A prison camp and the Road of Death.

Camps were built every 5-7 kilometers along the railway line according to a set design. A barbed-wire fence marked out a 200 x 200-meter square with watchtowers at the corners. Two rows of barracks formed the main street, which led from the dining hall to the gate, where there was a checkpoint, and then on to the railway line. Each camp contained about 500 prisoners, in seven or eight barracks, as well as a bakery, a bathhouse and isolation cells. Beyond the wire were the guards' houses and warehouses for materials and tools.

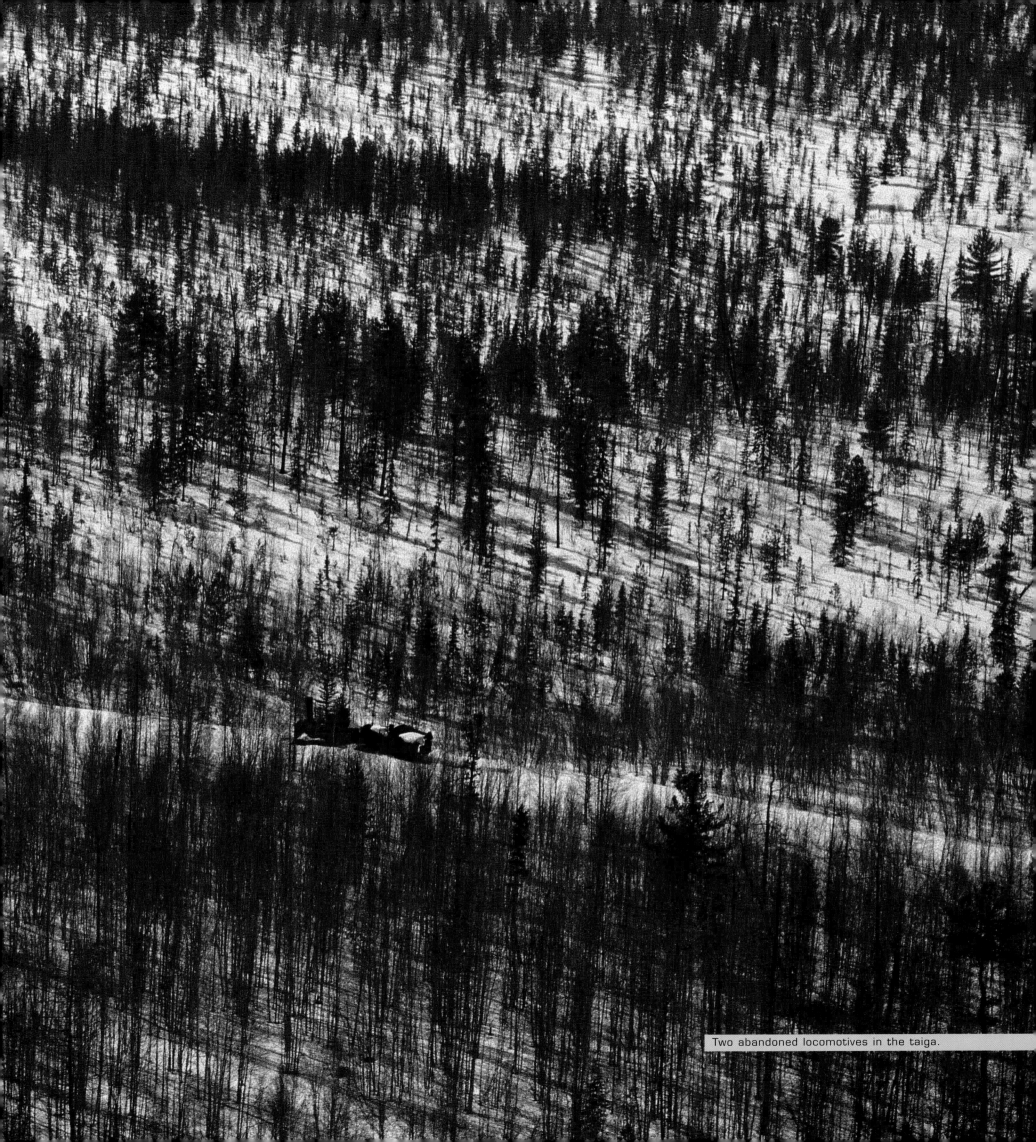

Two abandoned locomotives in the taiga.

Lithuanian Antans Siuksta and his son
at the old exiles' cemetery at Igarka. In
1948 his mother was deported to
Igarka, where she died in exile. Antans
Siuksta found her grave with the help
of a photograph taken at the funeral;
he had her remains exhumed and
returned to her homeland in Lithuania.

Tamara, one of the Siberian Selkup tribe, and her husband live
in old prison camp buildings. They hunt and fish on the Turukhan
River, a tributary of the Enisei.

Fisherman Boris Khochuev
is the only inhabitant of
Ermakovo, the former
headquarters of the eastern
administration of the Road of
Death construction project.

491

Tracks on the
Road of Death.

GLOSSARY

AK: abbreviation of *Armia Krajowa* (Home Army), clandestine military organization, active in Poland during the Second World War; members of the armed forces of the London-based Polish government in exile.

Chekist: official of the Cheka.

GUGB NKVD: abbreviation of *Glavnoe upravlenie gossudarstvennoi bezopastnosti* (Chief Administration of State Security). See NKVD.

Gulag: from *Glavnoe upravlenie lagerei* (Chief Administration of Camps). Name for Soviet security department that administered a gigantic complex of forced labor camps in the USSR. It was also responsible for the colonization (deportation and banishment) and the exploitation of labor, consisting of prisoners and displaced persons. The Gulag was created in 1930 and closed in 1960 but Soviet camps had existed since 1918 and continued to exist until the mid-1980s. They were administered by State Security departments under other names.

GPU: abbreviation of *Gosudarstvennoe politicheskoe upravlenie* (State Political Administration). Soviet security police created in 1922 to replace the Cheka; later renamed the OGPU or *Obedinnenoe gosudarstvennoe politicheskoe upravlenie* (Unified State Political Administration); responsible for arrests, executions, mass deportations and purges. The OGPU was absorbed into the NKVD in 1934.

Great Purge: A wave of Stalinist terror affecting all levels of Soviet society. Show trials were held in Moscow. Leaders of State Security (NKVD chiefs Genrikh Iagoda and Nikolai Ezhov who organized and conducted the Great Purge) and of the army (Marshall Tukhachevsky) were executed. The Great Purge began in 1934 and ended in 1938. It had reached a crisis point in 1937-38 when 680,000 people were shot according to the most reliable sources. The total number of victims remains unknown: estimates vary between two and three million.

Kedyw: acronym for *Kierownicto Dywerji* (Directorate of Sabotage), section of the AK that led an armed struggle against Hitler's occupying army by organizing sabotages and diversion tactics during the war. Detachments of the resistance carried out reprisals against Nazi officials, liberated prisoners and acquired weapons and money. The Kedyw soldiers fought during the Warsaw uprising.

Kolkhoz: from *kollektivnoe khozaiaistvo* (collective farm). Kolkhozes were created throughout the Soviet Union during the forced collectivization of agriculture that started in 1930; private property was eliminated and the Communist Party took complete control of the economy and social life in the country. Forced collectivization resulted in the deaths of at least fourteen and a half million people due to mass terror, famine, and the destruction of agriculture in the USSR.

Komsomol: from *Kommunistichesky Soiuz Molodezhi* (Communist Youth League), a socio-political organization for young people, 23 years of age and under, aimed at creating perfect communists.

Lubianka: headquarters of the security police located in Moscow. In the early 1920s, the Vecheka moved into a six-story building at No. 2 Bolshaia Lubianka St. whose main entrance faced Lubianka Square. From the 1920s until the collapse of the Soviet Union, the name of the security police changed several times, but its residence did not. The Lubianka building, also called the Big House, housed the offices of interrogator-investigators, a prison of 115 cells, and cellars especially equipped for torture and execution.

Mensheviks: members of the Russian Social Democratic Party. In 1903 they formed the second largest wing (after the Bolsheviks) of the Russian Social Democratic Labor Party in Russia. Hostile to the creation of the Marxist party that Lenin advocated, they joined the anti-Bolshevik camp after the October Revolution and were violently repressed by Stalin.

NKVD: *Narodny Komissariat Vnutrennikh Del* (People's Commissariat of Internal Affairs), national police organization first of the Soviet Union (starting in 1917) then of the USSR (1934-1946). The security police oversaw the police and criminal investigation departments and the Chief Administration of the Gulag and political espionage. Was Stalin's main political instrument for terror and genocide. In 1946 it was transformed into the Ministry of Internal Affairs of the USSR.

SR: abbreviation of Socialist Revolutionaries, members of a Russian political party seeking to overthrow the tsar and establish a democratic republic in Russia. After the revolution of February 1917, the SR party was the most powerful political party in Russia; after the October revolution, it headed the anti-Bolshevik movement. In July 1918, on Lenin's orders, the entire central committee of the SR party was arrested; its most prominent members were summarily shot, and the party was declared illegal.

NKVD troika: Common name for a committee of three NKVD officers; created to conduct limited police investigations and sentence prisoners to deportation, confinement in a Gulag camp, or summary execution.

Vecheka: *Vserossiiskaia Chrezvichainaia Komissia* (All-Russia Extraordinary Commission), Soviet security police founded by Lenin in 1917 and commonly called the Cheka. The number of victims remains unknown, but it reached as high as several hundred thousand. In 1922 the Vecheka became the GPU.

VKP(b): *Vsessoiuznaia kommunisticheskaia partia* (bolshevikov), the All-Russia Communist (Bolshevik) Party.

Zek: Prisoner in camp jargon, but also in contemporary Russian. Neologism created from z/k, an abbreviation of zakliuchenny (prisoner).

INDEX

PHOTO CREDITS

All the documentary photographs were taken from Tomasz Kizny's collection on the Gulag camps that he had assembled during fifteen years of research in Poland, the USSR, and Russia. They were acquired from different sources: the private archives of former Gulag prisoners and officials, as well as from various institutions and archives in the former Soviet Union and later, Russia.

The authors of the documentary photographs are unknown, with the exception of Stanislaw Kialka, former prisoner of Vorkutlag. He was the author of the photographs in the chapter on Vorkuta (pages 380-381, 385, 386, 387, 388, 390-391, 397). Some of the photographs in the chapter on Solovki were borrowed from Yury Brodsky's book *Solovki. Twenty Years of Special Purpose* and others from frames of the documentary film Solovki, commissioned by the authorities. It was shot in 1927-28 by the Sovkino film crew. The director was A. A. Cherkassov and the chief cameraman G. S. Savchenko.

The photographic and filmic documentation of the White Sea Canal construction site was ensured by the Foto-kino-buro, which was specially created for this purpose and headed by Alexandr Lemberg, who was probably an OGPU official. The photography section, which used several photographers, was run by a prisoner, Edmund Fiodorwicz, but we don't know whether he also took photographs himself. One of the Foto-kino-buro photographers serving a sentence at Belbaltlag at that time might have been Alexandr Bulla, son of the well-known St. Petersburg photographer, Karl Bulla.

The photographer of the OGPU Vaigach Expedition was probably Boris Ottle, who was condemned to ten years in a camp for photographing the destruction of the Holy Trinity Cathedral in Arkhanglesk, which was ordered by the authorities. The leader of the expedition, Fiodor Eikhmans, took photographs himself.

The documentary photographs of the construction of the Road of Death were largely borrowed from the album of the chief engineer Ivan Tarintsev.

The names of the photographers are [otherwise largely] unknown. The copyright on all the photographs whose authors have not been identified belongs to Tomasz Kizny.

All the recent photographs were taken by Tomasz Kizny between 1990 and 2002.

p.30 Gulag camp administrations in the USSR.